JO.

The Sea People

Copyright © 2025 by Joseph Malott

All rights reserved. No part of this publication may be reproduced, stored or transmitted in any form or by any means, electronic, mechanical, photocopying, recording, scanning, or otherwise without written permission from the publisher. It is illegal to copy this book, post it to a website, or distribute it by any other means without permission.

Joseph Malott has no responsibility for the persistence or accuracy of URLs for external or third-party Internet Websites referred to in this publication and does not guarantee that any content on such Websites is, or will remain, accurate or appropriate.

Designations used by companies to distinguish their products are often claimed as trademarks. All brand names and product names used in this book and on its cover are trade names, service marks, trademarks and registered trademarks of their respective owners. The publishers and the book are not associated with any product or vendor mentioned in this book. None of the companies referenced within the book have endorsed the book.

Cover by Dani Olette

First edition

This book was professionally typeset on Reedsy. Find out more at reedsy.com

Contents

Introduction   v
The Inscription   xix

I   Part One

1   The Great Club   3
2   The Palace and the Scribe   16
3   Masters of the Wine-Dark Sea   28
4   The Storm Gathers   42

II   The Storm Gathers

5   The Earth Groans and the Sky Burns   59
6   Rust in the Bronze Machine   71
7   Whispers from the West   79

III   The Great Unraveling

8   The Last Letter from Ugarit   93
9   The End of the Heroes   105
10   The Phantom Empire   117
11   The Face of the Enemy   129

IV   Out of the Ashes

12 The Long Shadow	145
13 The Raiders Settle Down: The Philistines	157
14 The God from the Mountains	168
15 Masters of the Alphabet: The Phoenician Dawn	179

Conclusion	192
Dramatis Personae	197
Timeline of Collapse	203
A Curated Visual Archive for the Late Bronze Age Collapse	209
A Note On Sources	228

Introduction

The Mouth of the Nile, Eighth Year of the Reign of Ramesses III (circa 1178 B.C.)

The air, thick with the damp breath of the Delta, tasted of salt and fear. Keni, Scribe of the Third Division, clutched the papyrus roll in his satchel as if it were a talisman against the horrors the morning promised. The ink inside was dry, the reed pens silent, but his mind was already composing the chronicle of this day, a task that felt both monumental and utterly futile. What words could capture the end of the world?

He stood on the packed-earth bank of the Pelusiac branch of the Great River, a man of letters and lists marooned in a sea of muscle and bronze. All around him, the might of the Two Lands was arrayed in suffocating numbers. Thousands of Egyptian infantrymen stood in disciplined ranks, their linen kilts stark white against the dark, fertile soil. Their polished spearheads, shaped like willow leaves, pricked the hazy dawn sky, a forest of deadly metal. Sunlight glinted off the broad, ox-hide shields and the intricate scales of the commanders' corselets. To his left and right, stretching as far as the eye could see, were the archers. They were the wall upon which the coming wave would break. Each man carried a powerful composite bow and quivers heavy with reed arrows fletched with the feathers of eagles and vultures.

Keni was not a soldier. His hands, accustomed to the smooth caress of papyrus and the precise grip of a pen, now felt clumsy and weak around the hilt of the short sword, the khepesh, that had been pressed upon him. Its curved, sickle-like blade felt alien and thirsty. He was attached to the command barge of Neb-Senu, a towering Nubian general whose scarred face was a map of past campaigns in Libya and Syria. Keni's official duty was to record the general's commands, the disposition of troops, and the tally of the slain—both ours and theirs. His unofficial duty, known only to himself, was to simply survive.

The waiting was a unique form of torture. For three days they had waited, camped along this strategic artery of the Nile, the gateway to the heart of Egypt. The silence of the dawn was unnatural, broken only by the nervous cough of a soldier, the creak of a leather strap, or the distant, mournful cry of an ibis wading through the reeds. The river itself seemed to be holding its breath. The usual traffic of merchant skiffs and fishing boats was gone, the waterways swept clean by order of the Pharaoh, Life, Prosperity, Health!

Pharaoh. Ramesses III, the Living Horus, was here. Not on this stretch of the bank, but at the strategic heart of the vast military web he had woven, his presence a divine assurance of victory. But Keni, who had read the panicked dispatches from the coast, who had seen the gaunt faces of refugees from the north, felt the divine assurance beginning to fray.

For a generation, the stories had been trickling in, whispers that turned to panicked shouts. They came from the sea, from the Great Green, as the Egyptians called the Mediterranean. At first, they were tales heard in the taverns of port cities like Per-Rameses, stories from the crews of Hittite and Alashiyan trading ships. A coastal town in the Lukka lands, gone. A Mycenaean citadel, a place of cyclopean walls and legendary kings, burned to the ground, its people vanished. Then the news became more dire. The great empire of the Hittites, our eternal rivals, the other superpower of the world with whom we had fought the legendary Battle of Kadesh—they were gone. Not defeated, not conquered. They had simply… ceased. Their mighty capital of Hattusa was a ruin. The city of Ugarit, the glittering jewel of the Syrian coast, a nexus of trade and culture, had sent a final, desperate letter etched on a clay tablet, a plea for help against an enemy from the sea, before it too was consumed by fire. The tablet had been found in the kiln where it was being baked when the city fell.

These destroyers, these ghosts, had no single name. The Hittite letters called them one thing, the Ugaritic scribes another. But here in Egypt, as the reports consolidated into a single, terrifying threat, they had been given a collective title, one that spoke of their alien origin and their implacable nature: the n3 ḫ3s.wt n p3 ym. The Foreign Peoples of the Sea.

"They are not like the Libyans," Neb-Senu had told his officers the night before, his voice a low rumble like stones grinding together. Keni, dutifully taking notes, had felt a chill that had nothing to do with the night air. "The Libyans fight for plunder, for cattle. They can be beaten and they will retreat to their deserts. The Hittites fought for power, for territory.

We understood them. We made treaties with them."

The general had paused, his gaze sweeping over the flickering lamps. "These... people... do not retreat. They do not negotiate. They burn the fields they conquer and salt the earth. They do not come for tribute. They come for the land itself. They come to replace us."

Now, in the tense quiet of the dawn, Keni understood. This was not a battle for a border or for a mine. This was a battle for the existence of Egypt itself, for the continuation of a culture that believed itself to be eternal, blessed by the gods and nourished by the predictable, life-giving rhythm of the Nile.

A ripple of movement went through the ranks. A cry went up from the watchtower nearest the sea, a long, sustained note from a horn that sounded less like a call to arms and more like a wail of despair.

Keni's heart hammered against his ribs. He scrambled up the muddy bank for a better view, his sandals slipping in the slick soil. He shielded his eyes against the rising sun, a great orb of molten copper that was just now clearing the horizon.

And then he saw them.

The sea, where it met the mouth of the river, was black with ships.

It was not their number alone that caused a collective gasp to be drawn from the Egyptian host, but their otherness. These were not the sleek, elegant vessels of Egypt or the sturdy, curved merchantmen of the Levant. These were broad, heavy-looking ships, with high, menacing prows carved into the shapes of ferocious birds of prey. Their single, square sails were dark and patched. But what was most shocking, what sent a wave of true dread through Keni's scholarly soul, was that they were packed to the gunwales not just with warriors, but with families.

He could see them clearly now as they drew closer, propelled by oars and the morning breeze. Throngs of men stood on the decks, a terrifyingly motley army. Some wore horned helmets, disturbingly similar to those worn by the Sherden mercenaries who, ironically, now served in Pharaoh's own bodyguard. Others wore tall, feathered headdresses that gave them a bizarre, inhuman silhouette. They carried round shields, unlike the Egyptians' rectangular ones, and long, straight swords.

But behind the warriors, huddled amid the supplies and gear, were women and children. Keni could see their pale, frightened faces turned toward the shore, toward the land they meant to take. And on the decks of the larger ships were heavy, two-wheeled oxcarts, laden with household goods. This was not an invasion force. This was a migration. A nation, or a coalition of nations, afloat, their lands behind them lost or abandoned, their only hope the rich, black soil of Keni's home.

This was the source of the terror. A raiding army can be defeated, its remnants scattered. But how do you defeat a people who have nowhere to go back to? Their desperation would be a weapon far more potent than any bronze sword.

"Hold your positions!" Neb-Senu's voice boomed, cutting through the rising murmur of the troops. "Let them enter the throat!"

Keni understood the strategy. It was brilliant, born of Pharaoh's cunning. The Egyptians were not meeting them on the open sea, where the invaders' seamanship might be superior. They had lured them into the narrow, reed-choked channels of the Delta, a killing ground of Pharaoh's own choosing. The Egyptian fleet, smaller, more maneuverable ships, lay hidden in the labyrinthine waterways, ready to spring the trap. The banks were lined with the deadliest archers in the world.

The lead Sea Peoples' ship, a vessel with a terrifyingly sharp, swan-like prow, crossed the invisible line into the river's mouth. Then another, and another. They came on with a dreadful confidence, a fleet of wolves entering a canyon. Perhaps they mistook the lack of opposition for cowardice. Or perhaps they had no choice but to press forward.

Keni watched, his knuckles white on the railing of the command barge. He saw a warrior on the lead ship, a giant of a man with a wild red beard and a helmet adorned with two sharp, bronze horns. The man raised his sword and roared a challenge in a guttural language that grated on the ear. The cry was picked up by a thousand other throats, a discordant, savage symphony that seemed to suck the very air from Keni's lungs.

It was then that Neb-Senu gave the signal.

A single, high-pitched trumpet blast cut through the din.

And all hell broke loose.

From hidden canals and reed beds to the left and right, the Egyptian fleet surged forth. Their ships were low and agile, with lion-headed prows that symbolized the power of the Pharaoh. They were not aiming for a conventional ship-to-ship battle. They drove straight for the flanks of the Sea Peoples' flotilla, their primary crews not marines, but rowers, pulling with all their might to build momentum.

Simultaneously, the archers on the banks drew their bows as one. The sound was like the sharp intake of breath of a giant, a taut creak of wood and sinew on a colossal scale.

"Archers!" a commander screamed. "Volley!"

There was a sound like a thousand giant sails ripping at once, a deep, resonant thrum that vibrated in Keni's bones. The sky went dark. A cloud of arrows, so dense it seemed to blot out the sun, rose in a graceful, horrifying arc, hung for a moment at its apex, and then plunged down into the packed decks of the enemy ships.

The effect was devastating. The Sea Peoples had shields, but they had no answer for an attack of this magnitude, coming from above and from the sides. The first volley was a storm of piercing death. Screams tore through the air, no longer war cries, but shrieks of agony and shock. Men clutched at shafts buried in their chests and throats, falling where they stood. The disciplined Egyptian archers were already nocking their second arrows before the first had found their marks.

Keni watched, mesmerized and sickened. He saw one of the oxcarts, the symbol of the invaders' desperate migration, riddled with arrows, the beasts that pulled it collapsing in a tangle of limbs and leather. A woman fell beside it, her cry swallowed by the cacophony.

But they were not broken. Warriors formed shield walls, holding their round bucklers above their heads like tortoise shells, while others hurled heavy javelins toward the banks. A few thudded into the earth near Keni's position, and he flinched, the reality of his own mortality a sudden, cold shock.

The Egyptian fleet slammed into the enemy ships. But they did not try to board. Instead, grappling hooks on long ropes were thrown, catching on the high prows and rails of the invaders' vessels. The Egyptian rowers, protected by marine infantry, dug their oars into the water and began to pull, not to bring the ships together, but to capsize them.

It was a brutal, merciless tactic. A huge Sea People ship, its deck still swarming with warriors, listed heavily. Men screamed as they lost their footing, sliding across the deck into the churning water. The ship groaned, the sound of its timbers tearing apart a sickening crunch that was audible even over the battle. With a final, lurching heave, it rolled over, throwing its entire human cargo—warriors, sailors, families—into the Nile.

The water, once green and brown, began to bloom with patches of crimson.

Another volley of arrows. And another. It was a machine of death, the well-oiled, perfectly organized Egyptian military grinding the chaotic, desperate horde to pieces.

But the Sea Peoples were fighting with the fury of cornered animals. One of their ships, smaller and more agile than the others, broke free from the melee and drove straight for Neb-Senu's command barge. Keni saw the faces of the warriors on board, their features contorted with a hate that was absolute. These were the Peleset, he thought, recognizing the tall, fluted headdresses from the intelligence drawings. They threw grappling hooks of their own, and the hooks bit deep into the barge's wooden railing.

"Repel boarders!" Neb-Senu roared, drawing a magnificent bronze khepesh whose hilt was wrapped in gold wire.

The Peleset warriors swarmed across. They were huge, powerful men, fighting with a terrifying frenzy. An Egyptian marine, a boy of no more than seventeen, thrust his spear at the first boarder. The Peleset warrior simply batted the spear aside with his shield, and with a single, brutal swing of his long sword, hewed the boy down.

Keni was frozen. The neat categories of his scribe's mind—'ally', 'enemy', 'casualty'—dissolved into pure, unreasoning terror. The battle was no longer a spectacle to be observed; it was a physical presence, hot and stinking of blood and sweat, and it was about to consume him.

A warrior with a scarred face and a wild mane of black hair locked eyes with him. He saw Keni not as a threat, but as an easy kill. The man grinned, a chilling, predatory expression, and pushed past a grappling Egyptian soldier to get to him. Keni fumbled for his sword, his fingers numb and clumsy. He raised it, but it felt as heavy as a stone block. This is it, his mind screamed. This is the end. I will die here in the mud, another forgotten name on a list of the dead.

The Peleset warrior lunged.

A dark shape moved with impossible speed. General Neb-Senu stepped in front of Keni, his own shield taking the brunt of the warrior's sword blow with a deafening CLANG. The wood and hide of the shield splintered, but it held. Neb-Senu didn't flinch. With a grunt that was all effort and deadly focus, he thrust forward, not with his sword, but with the heavy bronze boss of his shield, smashing it directly into the Peleset's face. There was a wet, crunching sound, and the warrior staggered back, his face a mask of blood, his charge broken. Neb-Senu's khepesh followed, a blur of bronze that hooked behind the man's neck and pulled him off balance, sending him screaming into the Nile.

The general turned his head slightly, his eyes still scanning for threats. "Scribe," he said, his voice dangerously calm. "If you wish to write the history of this day, you must first live through it. Stay behind me."

Keni could only nod, his throat too tight to form words. He pressed himself against the barge's central mast, making himself as small as possible, his useless sword held in a two-handed death grip. From this new vantage point, under the terrifying shadow of his protector, he witnessed the climax of the slaughter.

The Egyptian trap was complete. The Sea Peoples' fleet was a wreck. Dozens of their ships were capsized or captured, their crews struggling in the water. And the river, the sacred Hapi, the Giver of Life, had become the agent of death. Men who were not killed by arrows or swords were pulled under by the weight of their own armor. Others, strong swimmers, tried to make for the banks, only to be met by disciplined ranks of Egyptian infantry who waded into the shallows to finish them with spear and mace.

And then the crocodiles came.

Drawn by the scent of blood, the great reptiles of the Nile, ancient and patient gods of the river, converged on the scene. Their long, armored backs slid silently through the water, their eyes cold and primeval. Their jaws, which could snap a bull's leg, now closed on the limbs of struggling men. The screams took on a new, higher-pitched note of utter, final horror. It was a vision from the underworld, a divine judgment enacted by the beasts of the sacred river. Egypt itself was rejecting the invaders.

The fighting slowly subsided. The war cries of the Sea Peoples were replaced by the pleas of the drowning and the triumphant shouts of the Egyptians. The archers lowered their bows. The last pockets of resistance were being mopped up on the shore.

Victory. It was a total, crushing victory.

Keni lowered his sword, his arms trembling with exhaustion and adrenaline. He looked out over the water. It was a floating scrapyard of shattered timbers, abandoned weapons, and corpses. The bodies of men in feathered headdresses and horned helmets floated beside the bodies of women and children, their migration ended in this bloody cul-de-sac.

Neb-Senu stood on the prow of the barge, leaning on his shield, his bronze armor splattered with blood that was not his own. He surveyed the scene not with triumph, but with a profound weariness.

"We have broken them," the general murmured, almost to himself.

Keni found his voice, though it was raspy and thin. "We have saved Egypt."

Neb-Senu turned to look at him, and there was no joy in his eyes. There was something else, something Keni had never seen before in the face of the hardened commander. It was a deep, unsettling wisdom, born from the horror he had just orchestrated.

"We have saved Egypt today, Scribe," the general corrected him. "But did you see their faces? Did you see their eyes? They were not fighting for gold or for glory. They were fighting for a blade of grass to stand on. They came from a world that is broken."

He gestured with his sword toward the wreckage, toward the vast, empty sea beyond the river's mouth.

"We have killed the flood," Neb-Senu said, his voice barely a whisper. "But we have not stopped the storm that caused it."

Keni stared out at the carnage, the words of his general echoing in his mind. The victory felt immense, but also strangely hollow. The enemy was defeated, their bodies now food for crocodiles. But they were only the evidence of the crime, the bloody footprint left at the scene. The true culprit—the famine, the drought, the earthquake, the collapse that had uprooted these thousands of people and sent them crashing against the shores of Egypt—was still out there. It was an enemy you could not meet with a spear, an enemy that could not be stopped by a wall of archers.

Later that day, Keni would be summoned by the chief scribes. He would be asked to contribute his recollections, his lists, his eyewitness account. He knew that the story they would weave, the story that would be carved into the eternal stone walls of the Pharaoh's mortuary temple at Medinet Habu, would be one of unblemished glory. It would depict Ramesses III as a divine warrior, single-handedly smiting the chaotic foreigners, his strength alone preserving the perfect order of the cosmos. The official record would show a mighty king defeating a barbarian rabble.

But Keni knew the truth. He had seen the oxcarts. He had seen the faces of the women and children. He had felt the absolute desperation of an enemy with nothing to lose. He had stood on the precipice and looked into the abyss of a fallen world. And he knew, with a certainty that chilled him to his very soul, that this great victory was not an ending. It was a beginning. It was the moment Egypt learned it was no longer the unshakable center of the world, but merely another kingdom of men, huddled behind its walls, staring in terror at the sea, and praying that the storm would pass them by.

The Inscription

The story of Keni the scribe, the Nubian general Neb-Senu, and their desperate defense of the Nile is a work of historical imagination. It's an attempt to put flesh on bones, to breathe life into the silent, stone-faced figures of the past. But the battle they witnessed is not imaginary. The slaughter in the Delta, the strange ships with their bird-headed prows, the invaders with their feathered headdresses, the shield walls, the capsized boats, and the crocodiles feasting on the vanquished—all of it is real.

We know this because the man who ordered the slaughter also ordered it to be recorded for eternity. He had it carved, in breathtaking detail, into the walls of his gigantic temple. And if you know where to look, you can go and read it today.

Our journey to the primary historical document, our first and most important piece of evidence, takes us to the west bank of the Nile at modern-day Luxor, the ancient city of Thebes. Here, a bewildering landscape of tombs and temples sprawls under a punishing sun. But one monument stands apart, not just for its size, but for its grim, fortress-like demeanor. This is Medinet Habu.

Forget any quaint notions of a temple as a quiet place for

prayer. Medinet Habu was a multi-purpose beast. It was a royal palace, an administrative headquarters, a fortified town, and, most importantly, the mortuary temple of its builder, Pharaoh Ramesses III. In ancient Egypt, a mortuary temple was a pharaoh's spiritual engine for the afterlife, a place where priests would perform rituals for centuries to ensure his soul lived on in eternal glory. But it was also his final, monumental piece of self-promotion. It was a permanent advertisement for his greatness, aimed at his subjects, his successors, and the gods themselves. And Ramesses III had a lot to prove.

He was not Ramesses the Great, the legendary Ramesses II who had reigned for an astonishing 67 years and covered Egypt in colossal statues of himself. Ramesses III was a successor, a man from a different family line who had taken the throne in uncertain times. He lived in the shadow of his namesake and seems to have suffered from a severe case of what we might call "greatness anxiety." He named his children after the children of Ramesses II. He modeled his temple on Ramesses II's own mortuary temple, the Ramesseum. He was a king who desperately needed a legacy-defining crisis to overcome, a spectacular event that would allow him to claim his place among the immortal pharaohs.

Around his eighth year on the throne, the world helpfully delivered one.

The outer walls of Medinet Habu are immense. The first pylon, a gateway that looks like two enormous, sloping towers joined at the base, is over 200 feet wide and 75 feet high. The stone is a warm, honey-colored sandstone. And nearly every square inch of it is covered in carvings.

This is history as comic book, as blockbuster film, rendered in stone. As you walk along the northern outer wall, the story unfolds. The scale is overwhelming. Ramesses III, depicted as a giant, ten times the size of any other human, smites his enemies. He drives his chariot over the writhing bodies of Libyans. He presents bound captives to the impassive gods Amun and Mut. But it's the depiction of the great battle against the sea invaders that arrests the eye and forms the bedrock of our mystery.

The ancient artists carved the scene with furious energy. You can see the Egyptian fleet, their lion-headed prows symbolizing the ferocity of the king, trapping the enemy ships in the narrow confines of the river. You see the Egyptian archers, lined up in perfect, disciplined rows on the shore, firing volley after volley into the chaotic enemy flotilla. The water is a maelstrom of sinking ships, drowning men, and snapping crocodiles. The Egyptian soldiers are orderly, heroic, professional. Their enemies are a tangled, screaming mass of desperation.

Look closer at those enemies. The carvers took great care to distinguish them. There are the Peleset, with their distinctive tall, feathered or fluted headdresses, like a kind of rigid, warlike brush cut. There are the Sherden, with their horned helmets, each horn punctuated by a disk in the center. There are others, all with their unique armor and weapons. These are not generic "barbarians." This is a specific coalition of peoples, and the Egyptians knew exactly who they were.

But pictures are only half the story. Running alongside and above and below these images are thousands of hieroglyphs, the sacred script of Egypt. This isn't just art; it's a meticulously captioned, officially sanctioned press release from the desk of the Pharaoh. And its words are chilling.

The Great Inscription begins not with the battle, but with the backstory. It sets the stage by painting a picture of an international crisis, a world on fire. Ramesses, speaking in the grandiloquent first person, declares:

"The foreign countries made a conspiracy in their islands. All at once the lands were removed and scattered in the fray. No land could stand before their arms…"

Ramesses isn't just claiming to have fought off a band of pirates. He's saying that a league of nations, based "in their islands," launched a coordinated, unstoppable attack that wiped entire civilizations off the map. To prove his point, he then provides a casualty list, a roll call of the fallen that, to a historian, reads like a litany of the dead from the end of the Bronze Age:

"…from Hatti, Kode, Carchemish, Arzawa, and Alashiya on, being cut off at one time."

Hatti was the seat of the mighty Hittite Empire, Egypt's great rival. Carchemish was a major Hittite stronghold in Syria. Alashiya is almost certainly Cyprus, the copper-rich island that was the lynchpin of Bronze Age trade. Kode and Arzawa were powerful kingdoms in Anatolia (modern-day Turkey). Ramesses is telling us that five major powers, including one of the world's two superpowers, were utterly destroyed by this rolling tide of invaders. This wasn't a raid; it was an apocalypse.

The inscription continues, tracking the invaders' destructive path eastward:

"A camp [was set up] in one place in Amurru. They desolated its people, and its land was like that which has never come into being."

The phrasing is terrifying. Not just defeated, not just conquered. Desolated. Its land made as if it had never existed. This is the language of total war, of eradication. This is what the scribes in Ugarit, a city in the land of Amurru, were trying to warn their king about in those final, frantic letters.

Finally, the wave reaches the borders of Egypt itself. Ramesses presents himself as the world's last hope, the final bastion of order against a tide of chaos:

"They were coming, forward toward Egypt, while the flame was prepared before them."

And then, crucially, he names his enemies. He gives us the official cast list for this coalition of destroyers.

"Their confederation was the Peleset, Tjekker, Shekelesh, Denyen, and Weshesh, lands united."

This is the first and only time in history that this specific group of allies is named together. This is the birth certificate of the mystery we call the "Sea Peoples." The inscription goes on to describe the battle in triumphal terms, echoing the images carved beside it:

"I prepared the river-mouth like a strong wall with warships, galleys and skiffs… They were dragged, overturned, and laid low upon the beach, slain and made into heaps from stern to bow of their galleys, while all their things were cast upon the water."

It's a song of slaughter, a hymn of victory. Ramesses even includes the detail that his Sherden mercenaries—the very same people whose kinsmen with horned helmets fought in the Sea Peoples' coalition—were instrumental in the victory, a strange and fascinating detail we will return to later.

The case seems open-and-shut. A mysterious confederation of seafaring peoples emerged from the islands of the Mediterranean, destroyed every major power in their path in a blaze of violence, and then tried to invade Egypt, only to be stopped at the last minute by the heroic Ramesses III. Mystery solved, right? The Sea Peoples did it.

But this is where a good detective learns to be skeptical of a confession, especially one that is so self-serving. The inscription at Medinet Habu is not an objective historical report. It is a piece of masterful propaganda, crafted to make Ramesses III look as powerful and decisive as possible. He inflates the threat to magnify his own achievement. We are reading the event through the eyes of the victor, and the only victor left standing. It's like trying to understand the history of a gang war by only reading the press clippings of the last kingpin.

And yet, buried within the propaganda are details that ring true, precisely because they don't necessarily make Ramesses look better. The most important of these is the detail, shown clearly in the carvings, that the invaders brought their families and all their worldly possessions with them in lumbering oxcarts. The inscription confirms this, noting that they came with their belongings, "their hearts trusting that they would fill their bodies."

This is not the behavior of a simple raiding army. Armies don't bring their wives, children, and furniture to a battle. Migrants do. This single detail transforms our understanding of the event. These were not just warriors; they were refugees. Desperate, violent, and well-armed refugees, to be sure, but refugees nonetheless. They weren't just trying to conquer Egypt; they were trying to move in.

This brings us to the central, nagging problem of the entire affair, the paradox that sits at the heart of this book.

Ramesses III wins. The inscription is unambiguous. He saves Egypt. He throws the invaders back into the sea. He captures their leaders and enslaves their people. He is triumphant. According to the logic of his own story, the threat has been neutralized. The forces of chaos have been defeated. Order has been restored.

Here's the problem. Ramesses III wins the battle, but he loses the world.

Despite his glorious victory, the world that Egypt had known for centuries was gone forever. The great international network of trade and diplomacy—the "Great Club" of kings who wrote to each other as "Brother"—was shattered. The trade routes that had carried copper from Cyprus, tin from Afghanistan, and luxury goods from across the known world were severed. The mighty Hittite Empire never recovered. The glittering Mycenaean palaces of Greece were already smoldering ruins. A "Dark Age" descended upon the entire Eastern Mediterranean. Literacy vanished in many places for hundreds of years. Great cities became small, impoverished villages.

Even Egypt, the victor, began a long, slow decline from which it would never truly recover. The reign of Ramesses III was plagued by internal problems: massive inflation, food shortages, and the first recorded labor strike in human history. He was ultimately assassinated in a palace conspiracy involving one of his secondary wives and a host of high officials. His victory saved Egypt's borders, but it could not save its economy or its central place in a now-defunct globalized world.

The inscription at Medinet Habu, then, is not the solution to the mystery. It is the mystery itself. It presents us with a perfect suspect—the Sea Peoples—but the crime scene is far too large, the devastation too total, for them to have been the sole perpetrators. If Ramesses defeated the agent of chaos, why did chaos win?

The stone walls tell a simple story of good versus evil, order versus chaos, Egypt versus the foreigners. But the truth must be far more complex. The Sea Peoples were not the storm. They were, as General Neb-Senu might have guessed, just the first and most violent wave of a much larger tsunami, one caused by deep, invisible forces—of climate, of economics, of systemic collapse—that were far beyond the power of any pharaoh to defeat. The inscription at Medinet Habu is our starting point, our most valuable clue. Now, our investigation must begin in earnest, looking beyond the boastful words on a temple wall to uncover the story of how the whole world came to an end.

I

Part One

Before its fiery end, the Bronze Age was a glittering, interconnected world—the first age of globalization. Great kings ruled a system they thought eternal, yet its very complexity was its fatal flaw.

1

The Great Club

Imagine a club. Not a gentleman's club with leather armchairs and brandy, but something far more exclusive, more powerful. Imagine a handful of men, perhaps five or six at any given time, who control the known world. They are separated by thousands of miles of treacherous mountains, scorching deserts, and pirate-infested seas, yet they are bound together by a shared set of rules, a common language that most of their own subjects cannot speak, and a web of obligations, rivalries, and blood ties. They are the ultimate global elite, the board of directors for the entire Eastern Mediterranean. They are the Great Kings.

This was the political reality of the Late Bronze Age. For roughly three centuries, from around 1500 to 1200 B.C., international affairs were not a chaotic free-for-all. They were a carefully managed, intensely personal system of diplomacy, a "Great Club" whose members were the rulers of the era's superpowers: the Pharaoh of Egypt, the Great King of the Hittites in Anatolia, the King of Babylonia in Mesopotamia, and, for a time, the King of Mitanni in Syria. Other players, like the kings of Assyria and the Mycenaean warlords in Greece, drifted at the edges of this core group, sometimes petitioning for entry, sometimes disrupting the game.

These men ruled as gods on earth, but they corresponded like a fractious, high-stakes family. They called each other "Brother." They arranged for their sons and daughters to marry, forging alliances in flesh and blood. They obsessed over the exchange of gifts—gold, lapis lazuli, chariots, horses, beautiful women—as the primary currency of their relationship, weighing the value of each shipment with the precision of a jeweler and the suspicion of a pawnbroker. They bickered, they flattered, they complained, they threatened, and they schemed.

Their world, built on these personal relationships, felt stable, even permanent. It was a system designed to manage conflict, facilitate trade, and maintain a delicate balance of power. But it was also a gilded cage. Its very rigidity, its reliance on the whims of a few powerful men and the steady flow of luxury goods, made it profoundly vulnerable. The members of the Great Club were so consumed with the politics of their own exclusive circle that they failed to notice the deep, structural cracks appearing in the foundations of their world. They were busy writing letters to each other while the storm that would sweep them all away began to gather.

We know all this, not from grand histories carved in stone, but from a miracle of preservation. We know it because of a pile of clay, found by accident, that opened a direct window into the minds of these ancient kings.

The Lost Archives of a Heretic King

The story of the discovery begins, as these stories often do, not with a team of diligent archaeologists, but with a local peasant. In 1887, an Egyptian woman was digging for *sebakh*—the nitrogen-rich soil of ancient mud-brick ruins used as fertilizer—in the dusty, desolate landscape of Tell el-Amarna. About 190 miles south of Cairo, Amarna is a lonely place, a broad, crescent-shaped bay of cliffs on the east bank of the Nile. It is the site of the ancient city of Akhetaten, the short-lived capital built by the most controversial pharaoh in Egyptian history, Akhenaten.

Akhenaten was a religious revolutionary, a heretic who abandoned Egypt's pantheon of gods to worship a single deity, the Aten, or sun-disk. He moved his entire court to this virgin site in the desert, a grand and doomed utopian experiment. After his death, his successors furiously erased his memory, tore down his temples, and moved the capital back to Thebes. Akhetaten was abandoned to the wind and sand.

As the woman dug in the ruins of what was once the city's records office, she struck something hard. Not stone, but a cache of baked clay tablets, most about the size of a modern smartphone. They were covered in strange, wedge-shaped marks. Knowing that anything old might have value, she and her neighbors gathered up the tablets. They were eventually sold, trickling onto the antiquities market for a pittance. At first, scholars were skeptical, dismissing them as forgeries. The script was cuneiform, the script of Mesopotamia, not Egypt. Why would a pharaoh's archives be filled with hundreds of tablets written in a foreign script and a foreign language?

The answer, once the tablets were authenticated and translated, was astonishing. This was not a local archive. It was the state department's filing cabinet, the incoming diplomatic and intelligence correspondence for the kings Amenhotep III and his son, Akhenaten. The language was Akkadian, a Semitic tongue from Mesopotamia, which served as the universal language of diplomacy for the entire ancient Near East—the English or French of its day. A Hittite king in Anatolia, wanting to communicate with the Pharaoh in Egypt, would have his scribes compose a letter in Akkadian cuneiform. When it arrived in Egypt, the Pharaoh's own scribes, fluent in the international language, would read it aloud to him.

Suddenly, the silent world of Bronze Age diplomacy was given a voice. And what a voice it was. The 382 tablets found at Amarna are not dry treaties. They are raw, personal, and emotional. They are filled with flattery, gossip, anxiety, and greed. They reveal the intricate machinery of a globalized world, a world where a king in Babylon could complain directly to the Pharaoh that his new palace was behind schedule because the gold from Egypt hadn't arrived on time.

Reading the Amarna Letters is like listening in on the private phone calls of world leaders. We hear King Tushratta of Mitanni, his kingdom crumbling, desperately trying to maintain his status by reminding the Pharaoh that they are family. We hear Burna-Buriash II of Babylon express outrage that his merchants were robbed and killed in Canaan, a territory under Egyptian control, and demand compensation. And we hear the desperate, pleading cries of minor vassal kings in Syria and Palestine, men caught between the great powers, begging the Pharaoh for a handful of soldiers to save them from their rivals or from shadowy groups of outlaws known as the *Habiru*.

These clay tablets are our entry point into the Glimmering World. They show us the rules of the game, introduce us to the players, and reveal, in their own words, the passions and pressures that governed the most powerful men on earth.

The Messenger's Burden

To understand how this system worked in practice, we must imagine the journey of a single letter. A clay tablet is not an email. It does not arrive in an instant. It is a physical object that must be carried by human hands across a landscape filled with peril. The messenger was the essential gear in this diplomatic machine, a combination of diplomat, courier, and spy, whose own life was often as fragile as the clay tablet he carried.

Let us imagine a man named Teshub, a royal messenger in the service of the Hittite Great King, Šuppiluliuma I, one of the most cunning and ambitious rulers of the age. It is a cold morning in the high Anatolian plateau, circa 1340 B.C. Teshub stands in the great throne room of the capital, Hattusa, a city of massive stone walls and towering temples perched on a rocky citadel. The air is thin and smells of woodsmoke and damp stone.

Šuppiluliuma, his face stern, hands Teshub the dispatch. It is a tablet of carefully prepared clay, its surface covered in the dense, intricate patterns of cuneiform script. The message, composed by the king's chief scribe, is a masterpiece of diplomatic ambiguity. It is a letter for the Pharaoh Akhenaten in Egypt. On the surface, it offers condolences for the death of a minor royal, but beneath the boilerplate language of brotherhood and shared grief are subtle probes, testing the young Pharaoh's resolve, seeking to gauge the political situation in a kingdom that has turned inward with its strange new religion.

The wet tablet is placed inside a clay "envelope," another piece of clay molded around it, which is then sealed with the king's personal cylinder seal, rolled across the surface to create a unique, repeating pattern—an unbreakable signature. The entire package is baked in a kiln until hard, then wrapped carefully in linen and placed in a leather satchel. Teshub is also entrusted with gifts, the lubricant of all diplomacy. For the Pharaoh, a set of bronze drinking vessels inlaid with silver, and for a high-ranking vizier, a bolt of fine Hittite wool, famous throughout the Near East.

Teshub bows low and backs out of the royal presence. His life, for the next three months, will be dedicated to this single object.

The first leg of the journey is the most rugged. His caravan, a small group of guards and pack animals, descends from the high plateau of Hattusa, traversing the treacherous passes of the Taurus Mountains. Here, the threat is not armies, but bandits—the Kaska people, hill-tribes who have plagued the Hittite kingdom for centuries. The nights are cold, the path is narrow, and a single misplaced step could send a donkey, laden with precious goods, tumbling into a ravine.

After weeks of travel, they descend into the warmer, more cosmopolitan plains of Syria. This is a land of shifting allegiances, a political chessboard where Hittite and Egyptian influence collide. In cities like Kadesh and Aleppo, Teshub is a foreign dignitary. He is housed and fed by the local vassal kings, but he knows he is being watched. Every conversation is a potential intelligence leak. Does he seem confident? Do his guards look strong? News of Hittite strength, or weakness, will travel fast.

From Syria, the caravan turns south, following the ancient coastal road, the *Via Maris*. They pass through cities whose names will echo through history: Byblos, Sidon, Tyre. The air grows thick with the scent of salt and cedar. Here, the primary danger shifts from bandits to bureaucrats. At the borders of Egyptian-controlled territory in Canaan, he must present his credentials to Egyptian garrisons. His papers are scrutinized, his cargo inspected. A delay of a few days, waiting for the local commander's permission to proceed, is standard.

Finally, he crosses the harsh Sinai desert, the great arid buffer between Asia and Africa. For days, there is nothing but sand, rock, and a punishing sun. Water is more precious than gold. At last, he reaches the eastern branch of the Nile Delta, and the world transforms. Suddenly, everything is green. The rich, black soil, the lifeblood of Egypt, supports a civilization that feels ancient and overwhelmingly powerful.

The last leg of his journey is a boat trip up the Nile. He sails past endless fields of wheat and barley, bustling villages, and monumental temples that seem to have been built by gods, not men. After a journey of more than 1,500 miles, he arrives at his destination: the bizarre and magnificent new city of Akhetaten. Here, under the full glare of the sun god Aten, he is finally ushered into the presence of the Pharaoh.

He presents his tablet and the gifts. The Pharaoh's scribes will break the clay envelope, read the Hittite king's words, and begin to compose a reply. For Teshub, there is a period of waiting, of being feted and observed, before he must make the entire journey in reverse, carrying the Pharaoh's response back to his own king. He has done more than deliver a message. He has physically stitched the two kingdoms together, his journey a living thread in the vast, intricate tapestry of Bronze Age diplomacy. He is one of thousands of unnamed messengers who spent their lives crossing and re-crossing the world, the human conduits for the ambitions of the Great Club.

The Price of a Princess

If messengers and gifts were the currency of everyday diplomacy, the ultimate transaction, the highest-stakes deal a king could make, was a royal marriage. A princess was not a daughter; she was a diplomatic asset, a living treaty sent abroad to seal an alliance. Her body was collateral, her womb a vessel for producing heirs who would carry the blood of two royal houses. The Amarna letters are filled with the often-tense negotiations surrounding these marriages, which read more like trade deals than family arrangements. Kings haggled over the size of the dowry, the status of the princess in her new court, and the all-important "bride-price"—the lavish payment of gold and goods sent by the groom's family in return.

No story better illustrates this than that of Tadu-Hepa, a princess of the Kingdom of Mitanni. Her father was Tushratta, a king clinging to power in a state that was being squeezed between the rising Hittites to the west and the ambitious Assyrians to the east. His only powerful ally was Egypt, the world's lone superpower, rich beyond imagining. Tushratta's diplomatic strategy was singular: to bind himself so tightly to the Egyptian pharaoh that no one would dare attack him. He had already sent his sister, Gilu-Hepa, to be a wife of Pharaoh Amenhotep III. Now, he would send his own daughter, Tadu-Hepa.

Let us imagine the scene of her departure from the Mitanni capital of Wassukanni, a city whose exact location is still lost to us. Tadu-Hepa is perhaps fifteen years old. She has spent her entire life within the confines of the royal palace, a world of intrigue, luxury, and rigid protocol. Now, she is being sent away, forever. She will never see her father, her mother, or her homeland again. She is about to become a piece on a geopolitical chessboard, her personal happiness a secondary concern to the survival of her father's kingdom.

Her departure is not a quiet affair. It is the movement of a small army. A vast caravan is assembled to transport her dowry, a public declaration of her father's wealth and status. The official list, which Tushratta would later send to the Pharaoh, is breathtaking. It includes: one set of gold chariot fittings, two chariots plated in gold, teams of horses, a litter for the princess decorated with gold and lapis lazuli, gold jewelry of every description—rings, bracelets, anklets, pendants—inlaid with precious stones, dozens of garments of fine wool dyed in purple and blue, chests of carved ivory, bronze cauldrons, and an entourage of hundreds of male and female servants to attend to her.

This spectacular display serves two purposes. It is meant to honor her new husband, the Pharaoh, but it is also a message to Tushratta's rivals: *I am still rich enough, still powerful enough, to send a treasure fleet overland to Egypt.*

For Tadu-Hepa, huddled in her litter, the journey must have

been a terrifying blur. The familiar sounds and smells of her home would have given way to the endless creak of cart wheels, the shouts of caravan drivers in a dozen languages, and the dust of the long road to Egypt. What were her thoughts? Was she proud of her role in saving her kingdom? Was she terrified of the unknown old man she was being sent to marry? Did she weep for the life she was leaving behind?

Her father's letters from the Amarna archive reveal his own anxieties. He writes to the Pharaoh with a mixture of paternal concern and naked commercialism. He begs the Pharaoh to love his daughter: "May my brother have 10,000 times more joy from her than he had from her aunt... May my brother love her very, very much." But in the same breath, he complains bitterly about the bride-price. The gold shipment the Pharaoh sent in exchange for Tadu-Hepa was, in his view, insultingly small. He even accuses the Pharaoh's officials of sending gold that wasn't pure. "Let my brother not send me gold that has been worked upon," he pleads. "Let them melt it and cast it in your presence... so that I may not be angry."

The fate of Tadu-Hepa herself becomes murky. By the time her massive caravan arrived in Egypt, her intended husband, the old and infirm Amenhotep III, may have already died. It is widely believed that she was seamlessly passed on to his son and heir, the young Akhenaten, becoming one of his wives. Some scholars have even advanced the tantalizing, though unproven, theory that Tadu-Hepa is none other than the famous Nefertiti, whose iconic bust is the face of ancient Egypt. If so, the Mitanni princess, sent as a political pawn, became one of the most powerful and influential women in the ancient world.

Her story, and the countless other royal women like her,

reveals the human cost at the heart of the Great Club. Their bodies were the threads that wove the diplomatic tapestry together. Their personal fates were subsumed by the strategic needs of their fathers and husbands. They were the living price of an alliance, the most precious gift of all.

The Cracks in the Brotherhood

The world of the Amarna Letters, with its elaborate protocols and personal connections, can seem like a stable, well-ordered place. But reading between the lines, we can see the deep stresses that were already beginning to pull the system apart. The "brotherhood" of Great Kings was a myth they told themselves; in reality, it was a ruthless competition for status and resources.

The primary disruptive force during this period was the Hittite Kingdom under the brilliant and aggressive Šuppiluliuma I. While the Pharaoh Akhenaten was busy with his religious revolution, composing hymns to the sun-disk and building his new capital, Šuppiluliuma was on the march. He saw Egypt's inward focus as an opportunity. He broke the unwritten rules of the Club, attacking and absorbing the Kingdom of Mitanni, the Pharaoh's longtime ally.

The fall of Mitanni sent a shockwave through the system. Tushratta, the father of Tadu-Hepa, was assassinated, his kingdom collapsing into a Hittite vassal state. The carefully constructed balance of power that had kept the peace for generations was shattered. A bipolar world was emerging, with two superpowers—Egypt and Hatti—vying for control of the crucial trade routes and buffer states of Syria and Canaan.

The letters from this period reveal a system in crisis. The King of Assyria, a newly rising power in Mesopotamia, writes to the Pharaoh and cheekily calls him "brother," demanding a place at the top table. The King of Babylon is incensed, writing to the Pharaoh, "Why have you allowed the Assyrians, who are my vassals, to correspond with you? If you love me, you will allow them no further audience and send them back to me empty-handed!" The club was getting crowded, and the old members didn't like it.

But the most poignant and foreboding signs of decay come not from the Great Kings, but from the minor rulers, the city-state kings of the Levant who were sworn vassals of Egypt. Their letters are a chorus of desperation. The most prolific of these was a man named Rib-Hadda, the ruler of the port city of Byblos on the Lebanese coast. He sent over sixty letters to the Pharaoh, a frantic, one-sided correspondence that charts his city's slow-motion collapse.

Rib-Hadda's letters are a litany of disasters. He is besieged by a neighboring rival, Abdi-Ashirta of Amurru, an ambitious warlord who is gobbling up Egyptian territory while the Pharaoh does nothing. Rib-Hadda begs for help. At first, he is confident, asking only for a small contingent of soldiers to secure his city. "Send me a garrison!" he pleads, letter after letter.

But no help comes. The Pharaoh is distant, distracted. The Egyptian administration on the ground is corrupt and ineffective. Rib-Hadda's tone grows more desperate, more panicked. His lands are being overrun. His people are starving. He reports that his own subjects are beginning to turn against him. "All my cities have been seized," he wails. "Byblos alone is left to me… I am like a bird in a cage."

His final letters are heartbreaking. He is old, sick, and abandoned. He has been deposed in a coup and is living in exile in Beirut, still frantically writing to a Pharaoh who will not answer. "Let the king, my lord, know that Byblos, the faithful handmaiden of the king from the days of his fathers, is now lost." Rib-Hadda vanishes from the historical record, likely assassinated, a loyal servant sacrificed to the indifference of his master.

The story of Rib-Hadda is a microcosm of the system's fatal flaw. The Great Kings were so focused on their own prestige, their shipments of gold, and their grand rivalries, that they ignored the rot spreading through the peripheries of their empires. They saw men like Rib-Hadda not as vital parts of their imperial structure, but as annoyances, gnats buzzing at the edge of their consciousness. They failed to understand that the stability of the entire system depended on the stability of its smallest parts. A port city like Byblos was not just a vassal to be taxed; it was a crucial node in the trade network that brought cedarwood from Lebanon to the shipyards of Egypt. When Byblos fell, a vital artery was severed.

The Glimmering World was built on this network of arteries. It was a magnificent, complex organism, but one whose health depended on every part functioning correctly. The Great Kings, in their gilded palaces, acted as the brain, but they were losing sensation in their own limbs. The desperate cries of men like Rib-Hadda were the symptoms of a creeping paralysis they chose to ignore, a warning of the systemic failure that was to come. Their club, which had seemed so strong and exclusive, was about to discover that its walls could not protect them from the world outside.

2

The Palace and the Scribe

If the Great Club was the brain of the Bronze Age world, a network of powerful minds communicating across vast distances, then the palace was its heart. From the outside, these structures were monumental expressions of power, designed to awe and intimidate. The fortress-palace of Mycenae in Greece rose from a rocky acropolis, its entrance guarded by the famous Lion Gate, its walls built of stones so massive that later Greeks believed they had been set in place by the mythical Cyclopes. The sprawling temple-palace complexes of Egypt were cities unto themselves, forests of columns and towering statues. The Hittite capital of Hattusa was a mountain stronghold, a fortress on a scale that beggars belief. These were the residences of the god-kings, the stages upon which the dramas of diplomacy and royal succession played out.

But to truly understand this world, we must venture beyond the throne rooms and grand reception halls. We must go down the narrow corridors, past the sentries, and into the humming, buzzing, relentlessly organized engine rooms of the empire.

For the palace was not just a home; it was a machine. It was a central processing unit, an Amazon fulfillment center, a Pentagon command hub, and an IRS collection agency all rolled into one. This was the "palace economy," the intricate and profoundly brittle bureaucratic system that was the true source of the king's power. And at the heart of this machine, holding its every gear and lever in his mind and on his tablets, was the most important man you've never heard of: the scribe.

In our modern world, we are accustomed to the idea of an economy as a decentralized, almost chaotic entity, a sea of private transactions, cash, credit, and open markets. The palace economy was the complete opposite. It was a command-and-control system of breathtaking scope. In theory, everything belonged to the palace: every field of wheat, every olive grove, every flock of sheep, every vein of copper in the earth. The king, as the earthly representative of the gods, was the sole owner of the state's resources.

From the palace, everything flowed outwards. It distributed rations of grain and oil to the farmers who tilled its fields. It allocated bronze to the smiths who forged its weapons and tools. It provided wool to the weavers who produced its textiles. It sent out soldiers to guard its borders and laborers to build its monuments. And in turn, everything flowed inwards. At harvest time, the vast majority of the grain, wine, and oil produced in the kingdom was funneled back to the palace, not as a tax but as the rightful return on the king's property. This tribute, collected and stored in colossal storerooms, was the fuel that kept the entire machine running.

This system allowed for incredible feats of mobilization. It could focus the resources of an entire nation on a single goal, whether it was building a pyramid, equipping an army of chariots, or mounting a massive trading expedition. It was efficient, it was orderly, and it was, on the surface, unshakably stable. But it had a fatal weakness. The entire edifice was built on the assumption of predictability—that the rains would come, the harvests would be plentiful, and the sea lanes would remain open. It had no Plan B. It was a system perfected for a world without shocks, a world that was about to cease to exist. To understand its inner workings, and its inherent fragility, we must enter the scriptorium of a palace on the brink of its own destruction.

The Scribe in His Office

Let us imagine a man named Arimnestos. It is late afternoon in the southwestern Peloponnese of Greece, around the year 1200 B.C. Arimnestos is not a king or a warrior. His hands are soft, his shoulders stooped from years spent hunched over his work. He is a scribe in the service of the *wanax*, the great king of Pylos. His office is a small, windowless room deep within the palace archives, a space that smells of damp clay, olive oil, and the faint, sweet scent of old papyrus—a rare and expensive import.

Arimnestos is working on a *phoinikion*, a palm-leaf-shaped tablet of wet, pliable clay, about the size of his hand. His tool is a stylus, perhaps of bone or bronze, sharpened to a fine point. With quick, precise movements, he presses the stylus into the clay, making the complex little marks that form his script. This is not the elegant hieroglyphic script of Egypt or the grand cuneiform of Mesopotamia. This is Linear B, a spare, functional syllabary—a script where each symbol represents a syllable (like *ka, po, ro*)—perfectly suited for its purpose, which is not poetry or history, but accounting.

His current task is an inventory of wheels. A chariot workshop has delivered its monthly production to the palace storerooms, and it is Arimnestos's job to record the shipment. He incises the pictogram for a wheel—a simple circle with four spokes—and then the Linear B symbols for the word itself: *a-mo-ta*. He notes their condition: *ne-wa* (new), *po-ro-a* (old), *no-pe-re-a* (not serviceable). He counts them, makes his marks, and then sets the tablet on a wicker shelf to air-dry.

This is his world: a world of lists. He is a master of nouns and numbers. All day long, he and his fellow scribes sit in these small, stuffy rooms, their minds a whirlwind of meticulous detail. They are the central nervous system of the palace economy. A shepherd brings ten sheep to the palace; a scribe records it. The palace issues rations of barley to a crew of female textile workers; a scribe records it. A perfumer requests a specific quantity of olive oil and coriander to manufacture scented oil for the king's court; a scribe records the disbursement and will later record the delivery of the finished perfume.

Arimnestos is not simply a clerk. He is a vital cog in the machine of power. The king may decide to go to war, but it is the scribes who know exactly how many chariots are battle-ready, how many bronze spearheads are in the armory, how many rowers can be conscripted from the coastal villages, and how much grain is available to feed them. Without the scribes' lists, the king is blind. The tablets they create are the kingdom's memory, its operating system. They allow the palace to see and control its domain with a level of granular detail that is astonishing.

The scribes themselves were an elite. Literacy was a rare and difficult skill, learned over years of arduous apprenticeship. They likely enjoyed a high status, better rations, and exemption from manual labor. But their work was ephemeral. The clay tablets they used were not meant to last. Once the information on a tablet was no longer needed—once the yearly totals were compiled onto more permanent but now-lost materials like papyrus or parchment—the old clay tablets would be wetted down and recycled, their surfaces smoothed over for a new day's accounting. They were the Post-it notes of the Bronze Age, disposable records of a disposable present.

No scribe, as he meticulously recorded the number of wine jars in a storeroom, ever imagined that his humble list would survive for over three thousand years. And none could have possibly imagined the terrible circumstances that would grant it immortality.

The Last Days of Pylos

On a sun-drenched hill overlooking the Ionian Sea stands the archaeological site of Pylos, legendary home of the wise King Nestor from Homer's *Iliad* and *Odyssey*. For centuries, this was just a story. But in 1939, the American archaeologist Carl Blegen, following a clue from an ancient text, uncovered the ruins of a magnificent Bronze Age palace. It was a sprawling complex with a great central hall, or *megaron*, whose floor was plastered and painted with stylized octopuses. Its walls were covered in vibrant frescoes depicting warriors, griffins, and grand processions. This was the Palace of Nestor, and it was a perfect example of a Mycenaean palace economy in action.

Blegen's team uncovered vast storerooms. In one pantry, they found the shattered remains of over 2,800 drinking cups. In the oil magazines, they found giant clay jars, or *pithoi*, set into plaster benches, some still containing traces of the olive oil they once held. This was the physical evidence of the palace's role as a great collection and redistribution center.

But the most important discovery came from a pair of small rooms near the palace entrance. They were the palace's main archive. Lying on the floor, scattered and broken, were nearly a thousand clay tablets. They were all written in the strange, then-undeciphered script that Arthur Evans had earlier dubbed "Linear B" at the site of Knossos on Crete.

And they had all been baked hard as brick.

This is the central, poignant irony of the Linear B tablets. These ephemeral records, meant to be wiped clean, were preserved by the very catastrophe that destroyed the civilization that created them. Around 1180 B.C., the Palace of Nestor was destroyed in a violent conflagration. The fire that consumed the palace's timber beams, its vibrant frescoes, and its royal inhabitants, also swept through the archive rooms. It turned the soft clay of the scribes' daily lists into durable ceramic, firing them for posterity in the kiln of their own destruction.

When the script was finally deciphered in 1952 by the brilliant amateur linguist Michael Ventris—proving it to be an early form of Greek—the scribes of Pylos could finally speak. And their message was profoundly, chillingly mundane.

The Pylos tablets give us a snapshot of a kingdom in its final year of life, a bureaucracy running at full tilt, obsessively cataloging a world that is about to vanish. There are no histories, no poems, no letters between kings. There are only lists.

One tablet (PY Ab 573) records the allocation of flax to a group of fourteen women. Another (PY Jn 829) is a detailed inventory of bronze, listing dozens of smiths by name and location and specifying whether the bronze is "for spear-points" or "for sword-points." Tablet PY Un 718 is a record of offerings to the gods, a fascinating glimpse into Mycenaean religion. It lists contributions for a feast: "To Poseidon, one bull, four rams… to the 'Mistress of the Labyrinth,' one bull…" It shows the palace not just as an economic center, but a religious one, responsible for placating the gods on behalf of the entire community.

Reading these tablets feels like an act of archaeological voyeurism. We are peering over the shoulder of a scribe like Arimnestos, watching him tally up the banal details of his world. But as we look closer at the tablets from the very final administrative period, a sense of unease begins to creep in. The dry lists begin to tell a story of a kingdom under immense stress, a state frantically preparing for a threat it cannot name.

The most famous of these are a set of tablets dealing with the defense of the coastline. One tablet (PY An 657) begins with the heading: "Thus the watchers are guarding the coastal regions." It goes on to list groups of men, led by named commanders, stationed at ten different points along the Pylian coast. It specifies the commander's name—a man named *E-ri-ta*, for instance, is in command of thirty men—and their location. This is a kingdom mobilizing its defenses, setting up a coastal watch.

Another set of tablets (the "Oka" tablets) are even more ominous. They detail the movement of military detachments under the command of high-ranking officials. A typical entry reads: "The detachment of Tros, son of Aletes, is going to Ro-o-wa: 10 men from Oikhalia, 10 men from Kyparissia..." These are not just watchers; these are mobile military units being dispatched to strategic locations.

The most chilling tablet of all (PY An 1) is a list of rowers. It begins: "Rowers to go to Pleuron." It then lists men being drawn from various towns and villages throughout the kingdom. The formula is stark: "From the town of X, 5 men. From the town of Y, 10 men." This is a kingdom conscripting a fleet. But what is most telling is the final line on some of these lists: *e-re-ta a-pe-o-te*. "The rowers are absent." The palace is calling up men, but the men are not there. Is this a sign of administrative chaos? Or have they already been sent away on some desperate, unrecorded mission?

These final tablets are the last heartbeat of a dying kingdom. They show a bureaucracy functioning perfectly, even as the world outside its walls is falling apart. The scribes of Pylos, in their final days, were still making their lists, still counting their men, still allocating their bronze. They were doing their jobs. And in doing so, they left us an accidental, eyewitness account of a kingdom preparing for an invasion that, as the burn layer proves, it could not repel. The fire that preserved their words also proves their failure.

The Commercial Hub of Ugarit

Not every palace economy was as rigidly top-down as the Mycenaean model at Pylos. Some 700 miles to the east, on the coast of modern-day Syria, the city-state of Ugarit operated on a more complex and ultimately more resilient hybrid system.

Ugarit was a jewel. Situated at a crucial crossroads between the Mediterranean Sea and the overland trade routes to Mesopotamia, it was a cosmopolitan melting pot, a nexus of international commerce. Its palace was vast and luxurious, but it sat adjacent to a bustling port and a thriving city where merchants from across the known world—Cypriots, Egyptians, Hittites, Mycenaeans—lived and worked.

The archives found at Ugarit, unlike the homogenous Greek-language tablets of Pylos, reflect this diversity. Scribes here were multilingual, fluent in the diplomatic Akkadian, but also using a revolutionary local invention: an alphabetic cuneiform script. Instead of the hundreds of complex syllabic signs of Linear B or Mesopotamian cuneiform, the Ugaritic alphabet used just 30 simple signs to represent the consonants of their Northwest Semitic language. It was a streamlined, efficient system, a technological innovation born of the city's fast-paced commercial needs.

The palace at Ugarit still sat at the apex of the economy. It owned vast tracts of land, controlled the production of key goods like olive oil and purple dye (harvested from murex snails, a fantastically valuable commodity), and collected tribute from its subjects. But it also co-existed with a vibrant merchant class. While some merchants were direct employees of the king, others seem to have operated with a degree of independence, owning their own ships and warehouses, and entering into private contracts.

The Ugaritic texts give us a far richer picture of daily life and commerce. We have marriage contracts, deeds of sale for houses and land, and legal depositions. One fascinating text records a lawsuit filed by a merchant against a sea captain whose ship sank with his cargo. We can almost hear the voices of these ancient businessmen, haggling and arguing, their concerns achingly familiar to any modern entrepreneur.

This hybrid system, with its mix of royal control and private enterprise, made Ugarit incredibly wealthy. The palace grew rich by taxing the vibrant trade that flowed through its port, a far more dynamic source of income than simply counting sheep and barley. The cargo of the Uluburun shipwreck, that incredible time capsule of Bronze Age trade we will explore later, is a perfect illustration of the kind of goods that would have filled the warehouses of Ugarit: raw copper from Cyprus, tin from Afghanistan, ebony from Africa, Canaanite jars filled with terebinth resin, and Mycenaean pottery.

But even this more flexible system was not immune to the systemic shocks of the era. The palace at Ugarit was still the ultimate guarantor of security. It was the king's navy that was expected to police the sea lanes for pirates, and the king's army that was expected to defend the city from land-based attacks. And like Pylos, Ugarit's final, frantic archives show a system under unbearable strain. As we shall see, the last letters from the scribes of Ugarit are even more explicit and terrifying than the stoic lists from Pylos. They are the panicked cries of a city watching its own doom sail in from the sea.

The Brittle Machine

The palace economy, in both its Pylian and Ugaritic forms, was a marvel of social engineering. It allowed for a level of resource mobilization and central planning that built empires. But it was a brittle machine, highly optimized for a stable world and dangerously vulnerable to disruption.

Its first great vulnerability was its utter dependence on agricultural surplus. The entire system was predicated on the palace's ability to collect more food than its population consumed, creating a surplus to fund every other activity: craft production, warfare, temple building, trade. This worked wonderfully in good years. But what would happen in the face of a prolonged, severe drought, the kind of climate event we now know struck the region around 1200 B.C.? A single bad harvest could be absorbed. Two would be a crisis. Three or four in a row would be a catastrophe. There was no open market where the palace could buy grain from abroad. There was no insurance. When the central storerooms were empty, the system would simply stop. The rations would cease, the smiths would lay down their hammers, and the soldiers would desert. The heart of the kingdom would stop beating.

Its second weakness was its reliance on a fragile social contract. The vast majority of the population—farmers, laborers, herders—supported the tiny, literate elite in the palace. In exchange for their labor and the fruits of their land, they received security and sustenance. The palace protected them from foreign enemies and doled out rations in times of need. But what happened when the palace could no longer hold up its end of the bargain? When raiders sacked coastal towns with impunity and the grain rations failed to appear, why would a farmer continue to send his tribute to a distant king who was failing to protect him? The system depended on the consent of the governed, and when that consent was lost, internal rebellion was the inevitable result.

The final, and perhaps most profound, vulnerability was the information bottleneck. The entire, complex apparatus was run by a tiny class of literate scribes. Their specialized knowledge of scripts, mathematics, and administrative procedure was the software that ran the palace hardware. When the palaces burned, this class was either killed or dispersed. And with them, the knowledge of writing itself was lost.

This is precisely what happened in Greece. After the fall of Pylos, Mycenae, and the other citadels, the Linear B script vanished completely. It was so intrinsically tied to the palace bureaucracy that when the palaces disappeared, the script had no other purpose. It was as if, overnight, an entire society had its hard drive wiped. For the next four hundred years, the Greek world was illiterate. Stories like the Trojan War survived only in the fragile medium of oral poetry, passed down in darkness until the Greeks, inspired by the Phoenicians, finally adopted a new and far simpler technology: the alphabet.

The dry, emotionless lists of the scribes at Pylos are therefore more than just an inventory of a kingdom's goods. They are a testament to a way of life, a whole system of thought and control. They are the final, meticulous records of a world that valued order above all else. And they are the ultimate proof of that system's fragility, a quiet and orderly accounting of the contents of a house just moments before it was burned to the ground.

3

Masters of the Wine-Dark Sea

Homer, the great poet who sang of the Bronze Age from the darkness of a later, illiterate time, famously described the Mediterranean as the "wine-dark sea." It is a phrase of immense power and beauty, evoking the deep, purple-blue hues of the water under a setting sun. But it is more than just a poetic flourish. For the people of the Glimmering World, the sea was not a barrier that separated them, but a great, flowing highway that connected them all. It was their Internet, their interstate system, their Silk Road. While the palace economies we have explored were the great, static hearts of their respective lands, the sea was the circulatory system, the network of arteries and veins through which the lifeblood of civilization—metals, ideas, luxuries, and people—pulsed and flowed.

This was the first great age of globalization. A king in Greece could wear a necklace of Baltic amber, drink from an Egyptian cup, and wield a sword whose bronze was a fusion of Cypriot copper and Afghan tin. This was a world bound not just by the letters of kings, but by the bills of lading of merchants.

The intricate dance of international trade created a level of interdependence that was unprecedented. It made the world rich, dynamic, and cosmopolitan. It also made it dangerously fragile. When this network was severed, the entire edifice of Bronze Age civilization would come crashing down.

To truly understand the scale and sophistication of this globalized world, we cannot look to the palace archives alone. The lists of the scribes are invaluable, but they are abstract. We need to see the system in action, to feel the weight of the cargo, to smell the salt on the air. We need a single moment, frozen in time, that contains the entire world within it. We need a time capsule.

And in 1982, off the southern coast of Turkey, a young sponge diver found one. He found a ghost ship, resting silently in the deep, its final, precious cargo a perfect snapshot of the Glimmering World at the very height of its glory.

A Ghost from the Deep

The waters off Cape Uluburun are a stunning, crystalline blue, a paradise for tourists and divers. But the coastline is rugged and treacherous, a place of sharp rocks and sudden, violent storms. For millennia, it has been a notorious ship-killer. In the summer of 1982, a young Turkish sponge diver named Mehmet Çakir was exploring a steep, rocky slope deep underwater. At a depth of around 150 feet—a dangerous depth for a diver breathing compressed air—his eye caught a strange shape on the seabed. It was not a rock. It looked, he later said, like a "metal biscuit with ears."

He had stumbled upon one of the greatest archaeological discoveries of the 20th century. Those "biscuits" were copper ingots, the raw currency of the Bronze Age, cast in a distinctive "oxhide" shape for easy transport. Çakir had found the wreck of a Late Bronze Age trading vessel.

The discovery came to the attention of George F. Bass, the pioneering founder of the Institute of Nautical Archaeology (INA) at Texas A&M University. Bass was the father of underwater archaeology, the man who had transformed the field from treasure hunting into a rigorous scientific discipline. He and his INA team, led by his eventual successor Cemal Pulak, understood the immense potential of the find. A shipwreck, unlike a city buried over centuries, is a sealed context. Everything on it went down at the same moment, giving archaeologists an unparalleled, uncontaminated snapshot of a single point in time.

The excavation of the Uluburun shipwreck was a monumental undertaking, lasting for eleven grueling seasons from 1984 to 1994. It required more than 22,500 individual dives. Working at such depths is profoundly challenging. Divers could only spend about twenty minutes at the wreck site during each of their two daily dives before having to begin a long, slow ascent with multiple decompression stops to avoid the crippling effects of "the bends."

The site itself was a three-dimensional puzzle scattered down a steep, rocky slope. The ship's wooden hull, made of Lebanese cedar, was mostly gone, consumed by marine organisms over three millennia. But its cargo, a mountain of metal, glass, and ceramic, remained. The archaeologists had to work with the precision of brain surgeons, meticulously mapping, photographing, and tagging every single object before bringing it to the surface. They used underwater vacuums to gently sift the sediment for tiny beads and gold fragments. They injected plaster into the empty shells of Canaanite amphorae to create perfect casts of the organic materials—olives, figs, pomegranates—that had long since rotted away. It was a heroic effort of patience and scientific rigor.

What emerged from the deep was not just a collection of artifacts. It was the world in a bottle. The ship's cargo was so vast, so diverse, and from such far-flung origins that it single-handedly rewrote our understanding of the Bronze Age. It was the physical manifestation of the globalized economy, the hard evidence that proved the world of the Great Kings was supported by a world of daring, entrepreneurial mariners.

Unpacking a Lost World

The sheer quantity and variety of the cargo is staggering. Let us walk through the hold of this ghost ship and examine its treasures, for each object tells a story, each a thread in the web of Bronze Age commerce.

At the core of the cargo, forming the literal and economic foundation of the shipment, was the industrial metal. The ship was carrying over ten tons of copper, primarily in the form of 354 oxhide ingots, each weighing around 60 pounds. Chemical analysis of the copper confirmed its origin: the rich mines of Cyprus, the island kingdom known in the ancient texts as Alashiya. This was the oil of the Bronze Age, the essential raw material for everything from plows to swords.

Ten tons was enough copper to equip a small army, to produce roughly 300 bronze helmets and 300 bronze corslets, with thousands of spearheads and arrowheads to spare. This was not a local merchant's run; this was a state-level shipment of strategic material.

But copper alone is soft and of limited use. To create the hard, durable alloy that gave the age its name, you need to add about ten percent tin. And here we find the most astonishing evidence of the globalized network. The Uluburun ship was carrying over a ton of tin ingots, some cast in the same oxhide shape as the copper. For decades, the source of the Bronze Age's tin was one of its greatest mysteries. There are no significant tin deposits in Greece, Anatolia, or the Levant. The analysis of the Uluburun tin points to an incredible source: the mines of the Badakhshan region, in modern-day Afghanistan and Tajikistan.

Let that sink in. To make a single bronze sword in a Mycenaean palace, a smith needed copper that had been mined on Cyprus and shipped across the Mediterranean, and tin that had been mined in Central Asia, carried overland for thousands of miles on donkey caravans through treacherous mountain passes and deserts, likely passing through Mesopotamia and the port cities of Syria before it was even loaded onto a ship. This was a supply chain of breathtaking length and complexity, vulnerable to disruption at a dozen different points.

Beyond the raw metals, the ship was a floating catalogue of royal luxuries. Packed carefully among the ingots were 175 glass ingots, shaped like round cakes of cobalt blue, turquoise, and a unique lavender color. This was the earliest raw glass known in the world, and its chemical signature points to Egyptian and Mesopotamian workshops. In the Bronze Age, glass was a semi-precious material, as valuable as gemstones, its manufacturing secrets closely guarded by the great powers. A Mycenaean king couldn't make this beautiful blue glass himself; he had to acquire it from the Pharaoh. This was the material used to create exquisite goblets, beads, and inlays for royal furniture, a vibrant splash of color in a world of bronze and wood.

The reach of the trade network extended deep into Africa. The ship carried logs of African blackwood—ebony—a precious wood that can only have come from Nubia, south of Egypt. It also carried elephant tusks and a collection of hippopotamus teeth, the raw material for ivory carving, a major luxury industry. The presence of these goods confirms that the trade routes extended far up the Nile, bringing the exotic materials of sub-Saharan Africa into the Mediterranean economy.

The ship's hold was also a perfumer's dream. Packed inside about 150 Canaanite amphorae—the standard shipping container of the day—was a ton of terebinth resin, extracted from the pistachio tree. This resin was a key ingredient in the manufacture of luxury perfumes and incense, a scent that would have filled the halls of palaces and temples. The jars themselves were works of art, but more importantly, they were practical. Their distinctive shape, with a pointed bottom, allowed them to be packed tightly together in a ship's hold, maximizing space and stability.

And, of course, there was gold. Not in large quantities, but enough to signal the immense value of the cargo. The most spectacular piece is a small, solid-gold scarab bearing the cartouche of none other than Nefertiti, the famous and powerful wife of the heretic Pharaoh Akhenaten. Was it an antique at the time the ship sank, a treasured heirloom? Or a sign that the voyage took place during her lifetime in the 14th century B.C.? Scholars still debate its meaning, but its presence is a celebrity cameo, a direct link to one of history's most iconic figures. Alongside the scarab were pendants, beads, and scrap jewelry of gold and silver, likely meant to be melted down and reworked by palace artisans.

Finally, scattered amongst the grand cargo, were the personal effects of the crew and passengers, the small items that bring the human story to life. There were swords of Mycenaean, Canaanite, and even Italian design, a hint at the diverse origins of the men on board. There were tools for shipboard repairs: saws, drills, adzes, and chisels. There were fishing hooks and harpoons. In the remains of the Canaanite jars, archaeologists found the remnants of the crew's food: olives, figs, pomegranates, grapes, and almonds.

And there was one object, small and unassuming, that speaks volumes about the sophistication of these mariners. It was a hinged wooden diptych, a sort of proto-book, its two leaves held together with an ivory hinge. The recessed inner surfaces would have been filled with beeswax, upon which a scribe could write with a stylus. The book was empty, its message erased by time, but its presence is electrifying. This was a ship where someone was keeping records. The captain or merchant on board was literate, tracking his cargo, his accounts, his contracts, on a reusable writing tablet. This was not a voyage of illiterate pirates; it was a highly organized commercial enterprise.

A Motley Crew in a Bustling Port

Who were these men? The ship itself was of a Canaanite or Cypriot design, built with the shell-first mortise-and-tenon construction common in the Levant. But the cargo and personal items point to a mixed crew. The ship's anchors are a mix of large sandstone anchors typical of the Syrian coast and smaller limestone anchors common in the Aegean. The pottery includes vessels from Cyprus, Canaan, and Mycenaean Greece. The balance weights used for measuring goods came from all over the ancient world. It seems likely the ship was captained by a Canaanite or Cypriot, but had merchants and perhaps crewmen from the Mycenaean world on board as well.

Let us imagine this ship, a few weeks before its final, fatal voyage. It is docked at the great port of Ugarit, the multicultural crossroads we visited in the last chapter. The air on the quay is a thick soup of smells: the sharp tang of salt, the scent of cedarwood from the forested mountains, the stink of fish drying in the sun, the sweet, heady aroma of spices and resins being unloaded from a nearby vessel. The noise is a cacophony. The shouts of dockworkers, the bleating of sheep, the lowing of oxen, and the babble of a dozen different languages—Ugaritic, Akkadian, Egyptian, Hittite, Hurrian, and the guttural Greek of Mycenaean traders.

On the deck of our ship, let's call it the *Sea Serpent*, a deal is being struck. The captain, a man named Baal-Malik, is a Canaanite from Ugarit, a veteran of the sea roads. He is leathery and pragmatic, his eyes narrowed against the sun's glare. He is negotiating with a younger man, a Mycenaean merchant named Lykaon. Lykaon is sharp, ambitious, dressed in a fine linen tunic, his hair styled in the elaborate ringlets favored by the Aegean elite. He represents a powerful *wanax* back in Greece, a king who has an insatiable appetite for the exotic goods of the East.

They are not speaking Greek or Canaanite. They are speaking the fractured, functional Akkadian that is the common tongue of commerce, their accents thick but their meaning clear.

"The price for the glass is too high," Lykaon insists, gesturing at the heavy blue ingots being carefully loaded into the hold by sweating laborers. "The Pharaoh gives it to my king as a gift between brothers."

Baal-Malik snorts, a wry, cynical sound. "'Gifts' are never free, my friend. The Pharaoh expects a return. And my price includes the cost of getting it here, which, I assure you, was not without… difficulties." He discreetly touches a fresh scar on his forearm, a reminder of a recent encounter with sea raiders off the coast.

Lykaon knows the game. He nods, conceding the point. "Fine. But the tin. I need more tin. My king is building a new chariot corps. The smiths are screaming for it."

"Tin is from the end of the world," Baal-Malik says flatly, his voice dropping. "It is harder to find than a modest woman in an Egyptian tavern. What I have is what I have. The caravan from the great river was late. There were… troubles in the mountains."

This is the daily reality of their world. A war between Hittites and Assyrians a thousand miles away can affect the price of bronze in Mycenae. A pirate raid on a single ship can disrupt the supply of perfume for the Egyptian court. Their world is deeply interconnected, and they feel the reverberations of distant events in their purses.

They haggle over weights and measures, over the quality of the terebinth resin, over the number of hippopotamus teeth included in the price for the ivory. A scribe, a young man in Baal-Malik's employ, sits on a coil of rope, diligently marking down the agreed-upon figures on a clay tablet, the temporary contract for this portion of the voyage. Finally, they come to an agreement. Hands are shaken. Wine is brought out. The deal is done. The *Sea Serpent* is almost ready to sail west, its hold a floating treasure chest, a microcosm of the entire world economy.

The Technology of Trust

How could a scene like this even happen? How could a Canaanite captain and a Mycenaean merchant, from two different cultures with different languages and different gods, conduct business with any degree of confidence? A deal is only as good as the trust between the parties. In a world without international courts or credit cards, how was this trust established?

The answer lies in a set of invisible technologies, a shared infrastructure of ideas and practices that allowed commerce to flourish across cultural divides. The Uluburun ship carried the physical evidence for this "technology of trust."

The first and most fundamental element was a system of standardized weights and measures. When Baal-Malik and Lykaon argued over the price of gold or tin, they needed to agree on how much they were actually talking about. The excavation of the Uluburun wreck yielded a remarkable set of 149 balance weights, one of the largest and most complete collections from the Bronze Age. They are works of art in themselves. Many are made of hematite, a dense, dark stone, and are carved into animal forms: a reclining bull, a frog, a duck, a lion. Others are simple geometric shapes—domes, squares, circles.

Crucially, this collection includes weights corresponding to at least five different regional systems: Mesopotamian, Syrian, Cypriot, Egyptian, and possibly Hittite. The merchant on this ship was a master of conversion. He could conduct business with a trader from any part of the known world, confident that he could translate their local units into his own. This shared understanding of weight, based on established standards like the shekel, was the bedrock of all fair trade. It was the system that prevented a merchant from simply using a heavier stone when selling and a lighter one when buying.

The second technology was the **personal seal**. In a largely illiterate world, how do you sign a contract, mark your property, or guarantee the authenticity of a document? You use a seal. Two main types were used: the cylinder seal, a small stone cylinder carved with a unique design that could be rolled across wet clay to create a repeating pattern, and the stamp seal, which worked like a modern rubber stamp. The Uluburun ship had several, including a beautiful Mycenaean lentoid seal and a Near Eastern cylinder seal made of hematite.

A seal was more than a signature; it was an extension of a person's identity and authority. When a storeroom was sealed with the king's seal, no one would dare break it. When a clay tablet was authenticated with a merchant's seal, it was a binding agreement. The seal was a powerful symbol of ownership and accountability. Baal-Malik's young scribe would have used his master's seal on the contract with Lykaon, making it official and legally binding in the eyes of the merchant community.

The third and final piece of the puzzle was the **lingua franca**. While the merchants might speak a pidgin version of Akkadian on the docks, for official contracts, diplomatic letters, and legal disputes, the formal, written Akkadian language was essential. As we saw with the Amarna letters, it was the universal language of the elite. This meant that a contract written in Ugarit could be understood and respected in a court in Babylonia or a governor's office in Egypt. It created a common legal and administrative framework that transcended borders. It was the software that ran the operating system of international relations, ensuring that everyone, from the Great King to the humble merchant, was, quite literally, on the same page.

Standardized weights, personal seals, and a shared diplomatic language: these three innovations formed an invisible scaffolding that supported the entire edifice of Bronze Age trade. They were the practical solutions to the fundamental problem of how to trust a stranger. They allowed our fictional Baal-Malik and Lykaon to overcome their cultural differences and engage in a mutually beneficial transaction, confident that the deal was fair and the agreement would be honored.

The Final Voyage

Our ship, the *Sea Serpent*, laden with its worldly treasures, finally leaves the bustling port of Ugarit. It sails west, hugging the southern coast of Anatolia, a treacherous but well-traveled route. It is likely bound for the Aegean, its ultimate destination one of the great Mycenaean citadels, where the powerful *wanax* represented by Lykaon awaits his precious cargo. This shipment represents the fulfillment of his kingdom's needs for an entire season—the raw materials for his army, the luxury goods for his court, the exotic items needed as gifts to his own vassals and gods.

The ship is a testament to the glory and power of his world. It is a symbol of a system that works, a system that can draw upon the resources of the entire known world and deliver them to his doorstep. It must have felt like a permanent, unshakable reality.

But one day, off the cape of Uluburun, something went terribly wrong. Perhaps it was a sudden, violent storm, one of the unpredictable gales that can whip the Mediterranean into a frenzy. Perhaps it was a navigational error, a moment of inattention that brought the ship too close to the jagged rocks. The ship foundered and sank, plunging rapidly into the deep water. Its crew—the Canaanite captain, the Mycenaean merchant, the Syrian sailors—were all lost, their stories ending abruptly in the wine-dark sea.

The ship and its cargo, this perfect microcosm of the Glimmering World, lay silent and forgotten for 3,300 years. Its discovery has allowed us to reconstruct the magnificent complexity of the world that launched it. But its fate is also a potent metaphor. It is a story of how a single, catastrophic event can sever a vital artery in the global network. The loss of this one ship was a tragedy for its crew and a major financial blow to its owners. But what was about to happen to the Bronze Age was infinitely worse. A storm was coming that would not just sink one ship, but would break every link in the chain, wreck the entire fleet, and send the whole glittering, globalized world plunging into the abyss.

4

The Storm Gathers

War is a mirror. It reflects the society that wages it, revealing its deepest values, its technological capabilities, and its ultimate fears. The wars of our own age are defined by the invisible reach of drones, the cold calculus of cyber-attacks, and the gritty horror of urban combat. The wars of the Late Bronze Age were something else entirely. They were a spectacle. They were a clash of titans, an affair of breathtaking expense, aristocratic flair, and terrifying speed. And at the heart of it all was the single most dominant, most prestigious, and most revolutionary weapon system of its time: the war chariot.

The chariot was not simply the Bronze Age equivalent of a tank. To think of it that way is to miss its true significance. It was a synthesis of technology, wealth, and ideology. It was the ultimate expression of the palace economy's power to concentrate resources, the mobile throne of a god-king, and the terrifying instrument of a new, high-speed form of warfare. For over four hundred years, from the plains of Greece to the banks of the Nile, the fate of empires was decided by the thunder of its wheels. The men who rode them, an elite international brotherhood of warriors known as the *maryannu*, were the superstars of their day, aristocratic knights whose very existence was underwritten by the sprawling palace bureaucracies.

This was an era of formal, almost ritualized conflict between great powers. It was a deadly game, but one with established rules, fought for limited objectives like the control of a strategic city or the loyalty of a buffer state. The goal was not annihilation but supremacy, a demonstration of power so overwhelming that your rival would be forced back to the negotiating table.

Nowhere is this system seen in sharper, more glorious focus than in the monumental clash between the two superpowers of the 13th century B.C. On a single, bloody day, on the plains of Syria, the largest chariot armies ever assembled met in a cataclysmic battle that would define an age. This was the Battle of Kadesh, the Super Bowl of the Bronze Age, a story of ambition, deception, and epic heroism—or at least, a story that was masterfully spun that way. To understand Kadesh is to understand the zenith of this world of Chariot Kings, a world poised on the precipice, utterly unaware that its magnificent, expensive, and rule-based way of war was about to become terrifyingly obsolete.

The Ultimate Weapon System

Before we can witness the battle, we must first appreciate the weapon. The war chariot of the Late Bronze Age was a triumph of engineering, a marvel of lightweight construction and composite materials. It was the Formula 1 car of its day, and like a modern racing car, it was absurdly expensive, required a massive support team, and was only effective on suitable terrain.

Forget the heavy, clumsy chariots you see in old Hollywood movies like *Ben-Hur*. Those were Roman racing chariots, built for durability on a track. A Bronze Age war chariot was a delicate instrument of speed and agility. The frame was made from steam-bent wood, often elm or another tough, pliable timber. The floor was a woven lattice of leather straps, creating a springy, shock-absorbing platform for the crew. The entire vehicle was designed to be light enough for two men to lift, allowing it to be carried over rough terrain.

Its most revolutionary feature was the spoked wheel. The invention of the spoked wheel, replacing the solid planks of earlier carts, was a technological leap equivalent to the invention of the jet engine. It drastically reduced the weight of the vehicle, allowing it to reach incredible speeds, pulled by two specially bred and trained horses. The design varied slightly between the two great powers. The Egyptian chariot placed the axle at the very rear of the car, creating a highly stable firing platform for its primary weapon, the bow. The Hittite chariot, by contrast, placed its axle in the center. This made it slightly less stable but allowed it to carry a crew of three—a driver, a warrior with a spear, and a shield-bearer—turning it into a kind of mobile infantry shock weapon.

Every component of this machine was a product of the interconnected world we have explored. The wood for the frame might be imported from the forests of Anatolia. The leather for the suspension and harness came from the palace's vast herds of cattle. The bronze fittings for the wheels and decorations for the cab came from the fusion of Cypriot copper and Afghan tin. Even the glue used to laminate the different woods of the composite bow was a complex, time-consuming concoction of animal sinew and horn.

Only a centralized palace economy, with its vast storerooms and specialized workshops, could produce and maintain these weapons in any significant number. The scribes of Pylos meticulously counted their *a-mo-ta* (wheels) and catalogued their condition. The palace at Knossos on Crete had tablets detailing over 240 chariots in its armory, each with its own set of armor and team of horses. This was a state-level enterprise. No independent warlord or tribal chieftain could hope to field a chariot corps. It was the exclusive domain of the Great Kings.

The men who rode them were just as specialized. The *maryannu* were an elite, hereditary class of warriors found across the Near East. Their name itself likely derives from the Indo-Aryan word for a young warrior, *marya*. They were the nobles of their society, granted estates by the king in exchange for their military service. From a young age, they were trained in the complex arts of driving a chariot at full gallop while simultaneously firing a powerful composite bow—a weapon so strong it could punch an arrow through bronze armor. This required a lifetime of practice, a level of skill unattainable by a common foot soldier.

They went into battle bedecked in the finest armor the palace could provide: long, flowing corselets of overlapping bronze scales sewn onto a leather jerkin, and magnificent helmets, often crested with horsehair plumes. They were the Bronze Age equivalent of fighter pilots, a small, elite cadre of highly trained professionals who dominated the battlefield through speed, shock, and firepower. They were the king's ultimate weapon, and their primary role was to shatter the cohesion of the enemy's infantry, to ride down fleeing soldiers, and, most importantly, to engage in combat with their opposite numbers, the enemy's own chariot corps.

This was warfare as an aristocratic duel on a mass scale. It was a contest between the elite champions of opposing kingdoms, a spectacular and terrifying ballet of speed and death. And it was this form of combat that was about to reach its violent, bloody climax on the road to Kadesh.

The Road to Kadesh

The stage for our great drama is a small, unassuming city in the Orontes River valley of modern-day Syria. The city of Kadesh was a prize. It sat at a strategic crossroads, controlling the main north-south trade route and the entrance to the fertile Beqaa Valley. For a century, it had been the flashpoint in the cold war between the two great superpowers, Egypt and the Hittite Empire. To control Kadesh was to control southern Syria.

In the fifth year of his reign, circa 1274 B.C., the young and ambitious Pharaoh of Egypt, Ramesses II, decided the time had come to settle the matter once and for all. Ramesses, later known as Ramesses the Great, was a man consumed by legacy. His father, Seti I, had been a successful warrior pharaoh, and Ramesses was determined to surpass him. He was a master builder, a prolific father, and, above all, a brilliant propagandist. He needed a glorious, legacy-defining victory, and Kadesh would provide it.

That spring, he mustered the largest army Egypt had ever put into the field. It was a force of over 20,000 men and some 2,000 chariots, organized into four grand divisions, each named after one of Egypt's principal gods: the Division of Amun, with whom the Pharaoh marched, the Division of Ra, the Division of Ptah, and the Division of Sutekh. From the magnificent new capital of Pi-Ramesses in the Nile Delta, this colossal army set out on a month-long, 500-mile march up the coast of the Levant, a vibrant and intimidating procession of bronze, linen, and imperial power.

But Ramesses was not marching into a vacuum. The Great King of the Hittites, Muwatalli II, was his equal in cunning and his superior in experience. He was no stranger to the delicate dance of international power politics. Receiving intelligence of Ramesses's massive mobilization, Muwatalli summoned his own forces. The Hittite army was a multi-ethnic, imperial host. At its core were the elite Hittite charioteers, but its true strength lay in the eighteen vassal states and allies Muwatalli had called to his banner. The Egyptian records list them with a mixture of fear and contempt: warriors from Naharin, Arzawa, Carchemish, and even allies from as far away as the Dardanelles, the legendary Trojans themselves. Muwatalli assembled a force even larger than the Egyptians', with some estimates placing his chariot corps at a staggering 3,700, almost double that of Ramesses.

While Ramesses marched north with open, ostentatious display, Muwatalli moved with stealth. He concealed his massive army behind the high mound, or *tell*, of the city of Kadesh, using the city itself as a screen. He then laid a brilliant trap, a masterpiece of military deception designed to exploit the youthful arrogance of his Egyptian rival.

The Battle: Deception and Disaster

As Ramesses and the leading Division of Amun approached Kadesh from the south, his patrols brought in two local Bedouin tribesmen. Brought before the Pharaoh, the two men claimed to be deserters from the Hittite army. They told Ramesses exactly what he wanted to hear. The Hittite king, they said, was terrified of the approaching Egyptian host. Muwatalli and his army were still far to the north, cowering in the land of Aleppo, more than a hundred miles away.

Ramesses, young, overconfident, and blinded by his desire for a quick and easy victory, believed them completely. He did not send out further reconnaissance. Convinced that Kadesh was his for the taking, he ordered the Division of Amun to press forward and make camp just northwest of the city, while the other three divisions were still strung out for miles behind him, slowly marching north. It was a catastrophic error.

As the Division of Amun began to set up its fortified camp—the ox-carts forming a laager, the tents being erected, the soldiers shedding their armor in the afternoon heat—Ramesses had effectively separated himself from the bulk of his army. The Division of Ra was just then beginning to ford the Orontes River to the south, disorganized and completely unaware of the danger. The Divisions of Ptah and Sutekh were even further behind.

Meanwhile, behind the Tell of Kadesh, Muwatalli held his entire army coiled like a spring. He had allowed Ramesses to walk directly into the jaws of his trap. As the Division of Ra was at its most vulnerable, strung out and crossing the river, Muwatalli gave the order to attack.

Some 2,500 Hittite chariots surged out from behind Kadesh and slammed into the flank of the unsuspecting Division of Ra. The impact was devastating. It was a vision of chaos and terror. The Egyptian infantry, caught completely by surprise, had no time to form their shield walls. The Hittite chariots, with their three-man crews, acted as mobile battering rams, crashing into the Egyptian ranks, their spearmen stabbing and slashing at the terrified soldiers. The attack was a complete success. The Division of Ra broke and fled in a panicked rout, streaming north towards the flimsy security of Ramesses's camp, with the victorious Hittite chariots in hot pursuit.

The fugitives from the Division of Ra crashed into the camp of the Division of Amun, sowing panic and confusion. Moments later, the Hittite chariots were upon them. They smashed through the unfinished shield wall and swarmed into the Egyptian camp, cutting down everyone in their path—soldiers, servants, and even the Pharaoh's own royal household.

In a matter of moments, Ramesses's world had been turned upside down. From a position of supreme confidence, he now found himself isolated and surrounded, his leading divisions shattered, the rest of his army miles away. The Hittite trap had snapped shut. By all the rules of Bronze Age warfare, the battle was over. The Pharaoh was about to be killed or captured, and the Egyptian army annihilated.

Ramesses's Finest Hour (According to Ramesses)

It is at this moment of supreme crisis that the historical account becomes a legend. Our primary source for the battle is the "Poem of Pentaur," a grand epic composed by Ramesses's court poets and scribes, which he had copied and carved onto the walls of at least five major temples, including Karnak, Luxor, and Abu Simbel. It is one of the most detailed, and most biased, accounts of a battle from the ancient world. And at its heart is the personal, divinely inspired heroism of the Pharaoh himself.

According to the official account, as his men fled around him, Ramesses was left alone with only his personal charioteer, Menna. Despair washed over him. He turned his face to the heavens and offered a desperate prayer to his divine father, the god Amun.

"What is this, my father Amun?" he cried. "Has a father forgotten his son? Have I done anything without you? I call to you, my father Amun… for the peoples are countless, and I am alone, with none beside me!"

And the god, the poem tells us, heard him. Filled with divine strength, Ramesses donned his coat of mail, mounted his chariot, and charged. Not in retreat, but directly into the heart of the enemy.

"I was before them like Set in his moment," the inscription roars. "I found the mass of 2,500 chariots… and I plunged among them… I was dispatching them, and they had no place to flee… I caused them to tumble into the water, as a crocodile tumbles."

The temple reliefs at Abu Simbel depict this moment in

stunning, monumental propaganda. Ramesses is shown as a giant, ten times the size of any other man. In his chariot, *Victory-in-Thebes*, he is a whirlwind of destruction, his arrows felling dozens of Hittites at once. He is not just a king; he is a god, a force of nature single-handedly holding back the tide of chaos.

This is, of course, a heroic exaggeration. But there is likely a kernel of truth to it. In the face of total disaster, it seems Ramesses did not panic. He rallied his personal bodyguard and a small core of loyal charioteers and launched a series of desperate, furious counter-charges. He was fighting for his life, and his personal bravery likely prevented a complete collapse of morale.

But the real turning point of the battle was not an act of god, but a stroke of luck and a fatal mistake by the Hittites. As their chariots swarmed through the Egyptian camp, they broke formation. Believing the battle won, the Hittite crews dismounted and began to loot, grabbing the gold, weapons, and treasures scattered throughout the Pharaoh's personal baggage train. Their discipline dissolved in a moment of greed.

It was at this precise moment that a completely separate Egyptian force arrived on the scene. This was a force of *Ne'arin*, a Canaanite corps loyal to Egypt, who had been marching up the coast and arrived at the battlefield from the west, completely by surprise. They slammed into the disorganized, looting Hittites. Caught on foot and away from their chariots, the Hittite warriors were slaughtered.

The arrival of the Ne'arin saved Ramesses. It gave him the breathing room he needed to regroup what was left of his shattered divisions. The tide had turned. The Hittite charioteers who survived the Ne'arin's attack fled back across the river, where Muwatalli, watching from the safety of Kadesh, was forced to commit his reserves—another thousand chariots—just to cover their retreat.

By the end of the day, the battlefield was a wreck of shattered chariots and dead bodies. Ramesses had survived, but two of his divisions had been mauled. Muwatalli's elite chariot corps had been severely bloodied. The glorious, decisive battle had ended in a bloody, chaotic stalemate. The next day, according to the Egyptian account, the fighting resumed, likely a brutal, grinding infantry battle with no clear victor. Both sides were exhausted. Ramesses, having salvaged his army from the brink of annihilation, declared victory and began the long, ignominious march back to Egypt, leaving Kadesh and the surrounding territory firmly in Hittite hands.

The War of Propaganda

Who really won the Battle of Kadesh?

Militarily, it was a strategic victory for the Hittites. Muwatalli had successfully defended Kadesh and checked the Egyptian advance into Syria. Ramesses had failed in his primary objective and had been forced to retreat. By any objective measure, the Pharaoh had lost.

But Ramesses II was a genius not of military strategy, but of public relations. He returned to Egypt and launched the most successful propaganda campaign in ancient history. He did not describe the battle as a tactical blunder that almost cost him his life and his army. He framed it as his own personal triumph, a story of a lone hero, abandoned by his cowardly troops, who saved the day through his personal valor and his special relationship with the gods.

He covered the walls of Egypt's most sacred temples with his version of the story. The sheer scale and repetition of the Kadesh inscriptions ensured that, for his own people and for posterity, his narrative became the truth. The failure of his intelligence, the rout of his divisions, and the lucky arrival of the Ne'arin were all downplayed or ignored. What was remembered was the image of the heroic pharaoh, alone against a thousand chariots. He had lost the battle, but he decisively won the war of the story.

The true end to the conflict came sixteen years later. After years of further inconclusive skirmishing, the two empires, now ruled by Ramesses II and the new Hittite king Hattusili III, finally realized that neither could decisively defeat the other. Faced with the growing threat of Assyria to the east, they chose peace. They negotiated the world's first-known comprehensive peace treaty, a document so remarkable that a copy of it now hangs in the United Nations headquarters in New York.

The Treaty of Kadesh, inscribed on a silver tablet, was a return to the old rules of the Great Club. It was a treaty of brotherhood between two equal powers. It established a permanent, non-aggression pact, a defensive alliance against outside enemies, and, crucially, a clause for the extradition of political refugees. The two superpowers, after fighting the largest battle of their age to a bloody draw, agreed to go back to being brothers. The system, though severely tested, had held.

The End of the Game

The Battle of Kadesh represents the absolute zenith of Bronze Age warfare. It was the system working at its peak: two massive, centrally-controlled palace armies, led by their kings, deploying thousands of elite, expensive chariots in a bid to control a single, strategic point. It ended, after a period of propaganda and posturing, with a formal treaty that restored the balance of power. It was a magnificent, terrible, and ultimately stable way of waging war.

And it was already a dinosaur.

The entire system of chariot warfare was predicated on the palace economy that supported it. It was incredibly expensive, requiring vast resources, specialized craftsmen, and long, stable supply chains. It was also inflexible, effective only on open, flat terrain against similarly equipped armies. What would happen when the palace economies began to fail? What would happen when the flow of tin from Afghanistan was cut off? What would happen when the enemy wasn't another state army fighting for a city, but a desperate, migrating people fighting for the land itself?

The Chariot Kings were masters of a very specific, very formal game of chess. They knew the moves, they understood the rules, and they respected the prowess of their opponents. But a new set of players was about to knock the board over. These new enemies, the Sea Peoples, would not fight in ordered lines on open plains. They would fight on the sea, in the hills, and in the reed-choked marshes of the Delta. They would not use expensive chariots, but would rely on masses of infantry with cheaper, more democratic weapons. And they did not fight for treaties. They fought for survival.

The thunderous charge of the 5,000 chariots at Kadesh was the glorious, deafening roar of a dying world. It was the last great battle of an age, a final, spectacular display of a way of war that was about to be swept away by a storm that no king, no matter how great a hero he claimed to be, could hope to defeat.

II

The Storm Gathers

The Glimmering World was a marvel of engineering, but it had no shock absorbers. Its foundations, which seemed like eternal stone, were in fact brittle glass. Now, the tremors begin: the earth groans, the sky burns, and whispers of new enemies arrive from the sea. The system begins to fray.

5

The Earth Groans and the Sky Burns

For centuries, the Great Kings and their subjects had lived with a core assumption, a belief so fundamental it was rarely spoken: the world itself was a stable stage upon which the dramas of men unfolded. The gods might be fickle, the rival king ambitious, but the earth beneath their feet was firm, the rains would fall in their season, and the sun would ripen the grain. The rhythms of nature were the metronome that set the tempo for civilization. The palace economies, the diplomatic timetables, the very idea of a predictable future—all of it rested on the foundation of a predictable environment.

In the decades leading up to 1200 B.C., that foundation began to crack. The metronome began to stutter. The stage itself started to collapse.

The story of the Late Bronze Age Collapse is often told as a human drama, a tale of migrations, invasions, and systemic failures. But that is only half the story. Before the Sea Peoples ever appeared on the horizon, before the palaces burned, the world was attacked by forces far older and more powerful than any king or army. These were the non-human actors, the indifferent and implacable antagonists of climate and geology. The crisis began not with a declaration of war, but with the silent, creeping failure of the sky to deliver rain, and the sudden, violent shuddering of the earth.

To understand what happened, we must become scientists. We must leave the archives of the scribes and enter the archives of the planet itself—archives written in layers of ancient pollen, in the dust trapped in polar ice, and in the fractured, toppled stones of ruined cities. For it was a tandem assault by drought and earthquake that delivered the first, and perhaps fatal, blows to the Glimmering World. This perfect storm of natural disasters weakened the mighty empires from within, creating the very conditions of famine, desperation, and displacement that would soon give birth to the raiders and migrants who would finish the job. The Chariot Kings were masters of a game played on a board they thought was stable. They were about to learn that the board itself was breaking apart.

The Archives of the Earth

How can we possibly know if it rained in Greece in the year 1250 B.C.? The scribes of Pylos did not keep weather journals. This question, for a long time, consigned any discussion of climate to the realm of pure speculation. But in the last few decades, a revolution in paleoclimatology—the study of past climates—has given us the tools to reconstruct the environment of the Bronze Age with astonishing precision. Scientists have learned to read the subtle clues the planet leaves behind, turning lakebeds and glaciers into libraries of lost weather.

Our first port of call is the bottom of a lake. Every year, a fine layer of sediment, containing dust, soil, and pollen from the surrounding landscape, settles on the lake floor. Over millennia, these layers build up, creating a perfect, year-by-year record of the local environment. A team of scientists can drill a deep core from the lakebed, extracting a long cylinder of mud that is, in effect, a history book.

The language of this book is pollen. Every plant produces pollen with a unique, identifiable shape. By analyzing the pollen in each layer of the sediment core, scientists can reconstruct the vegetation of the surrounding area. A layer rich in the pollen of oak and pine trees indicates a cool, wet climate suitable for forests. A layer dominated by the pollen of grasses and scrubby, drought-resistant plants like those in the olive family tells a story of a much drier, more arid landscape.

Across the Eastern Mediterranean, from Greece to Syria, these pollen records tell the same, stark story. For most of the Late Bronze Age, the climate was relatively stable and moist, the kind of climate that had nurtured the growth of these complex civilizations. But starting around 1250 B.C. and intensifying dramatically after 1200 B.C., the pollen profile changes. The tree pollen plummets. The pollen from hardy, dry-land shrubs explodes. The forests retreated, and the landscape became a parched scrubland. This wasn't a single dry year; the data points to a period of prolonged, severe aridity—a "megadrought"—that lasted for decades, and in some regions, for over a century.

Halfway across the world, in the frozen heart of Greenland, another archive confirms the story. As snow falls on the

Greenland ice sheet, it compacts into layers of ice, trapping bubbles of ancient atmosphere, dust, and chemical traces from volcanic eruptions. Like tree rings, these layers can be counted to create a precise timeline. Analysis of the ice cores corresponding to the Late Bronze Age shows a marked increase in the amount of sea salt and mineral dust. This indicates higher wind speeds and greater storminess over the North Atlantic, a sign of a major shift in the atmospheric circulation patterns that deliver rain to the Mediterranean. The climate system was not just drier; it was more volatile and chaotic.

Further evidence comes from the slow, patient growth of stalagmites in caves. As water drips from a cave ceiling, it leaves behind mineral deposits that build up in layers, like a candle dripping wax. The chemical composition of the water in each layer, specifically the ratio of different oxygen isotopes, is a direct proxy for rainfall. Speleothems from caves across the region confirm the same pattern: a period of relatively wet, stable conditions giving way to a sudden and dramatic period of intense drought at the end of the 13th century B.C.

The science is overwhelming. Multiple, independent lines of evidence all converge on a single, terrifying conclusion. The peoples of the Late Bronze Age found themselves facing a climate event of a severity and duration that no living person had ever experienced. The predictable rhythms of their world had broken. The sky, which had always given life, now burned with a relentless, brassy sun.

The Hungry Letter

What does a megadrought feel like to a king? Abstract data about pollen counts and oxygen isotopes can tell us *what* happened, but it cannot convey the gnawing anxiety of a ruler watching his world wither and die. For that, we must return to the clay tablets.

Imagine the Hittite capital, Hattusa, perched on its high, windswept plateau in central Anatolia. This was never easy land to farm. The Hittite kingdom had always been more vulnerable to famine than the blessedly fertile river valleys of Egypt or Mesopotamia. Its power depended on the palace's ability to manage and store the grain from its marginal lands.

Now, imagine the harvests failing. Not once, but year after year. The spring rains come late, or not at all. The summer sun is merciless, baking the fields to cracked clay. The wheat stalks are stunted, the ears of barley thin and withered. The great stone silos of the palace, designed to hold years of surplus, begin to empty. The scribes' tablets, which once recorded abundance, now track a terrifying deficit. The palace can no longer provide the full rations to its soldiers, its artisans, its priests. The lowing of starving cattle echoes in the fields. The faces of the common people grow gaunt, their loyalty strained to the breaking point. The social contract is fraying.

A Great King, a man who called the Pharaoh "Brother," a living god on earth, was reduced to the most basic and humiliating of human conditions: he was hungry. And he was forced to beg.

Among the archives found at the port city of Ugarit is a letter. It is not from the king of Ugarit, but to him. The author is Šuppiluliuma II, the last known king of the mighty Hittite Empire. The letter is a desperate, urgent plea. It is a shipping order for 2,000 measures of grain—an immense quantity, perhaps 450 tons—to be loaded onto a ship belonging to a man named Shikila and sent immediately to a Hittite port. The tone is not one of a superpower issuing a command to a vassal; it is the plea of a desperate man. And it contains a line that echoes across the millennia, a cry of pure anguish that makes the climate data devastatingly real:

"It is a matter of life and death!"

This is the sound of a world breaking. The Great King of Hatti, ruler of a vast empire, whose armies had fought the Egyptians to a standstill at Kadesh, cannot feed his own people. He is forced to rely on emergency grain shipments from his vassals, shipments that must travel by sea, a mode of transport that was becoming increasingly perilous. Other texts confirm this was not an isolated crisis. The Hittite Queen Puduhepa had written to Ramesses II a generation earlier, complaining that she had "no grain at all in her lands." The Egyptians, blessed by the predictable flood of the Nile which made them more resilient to drought, seem to have been shipping emergency grain to the Hittites for years.

This was not charity. It was a calculated act of foreign policy. A stable Hittite empire, even a rival one, was a known quantity. A collapsing, starving Hittite empire on Egypt's northern border was a terrifying prospect, one that could unleash chaos across the entire region. The Pharaoh was sending food to his rival not out of brotherhood, but to keep the system from imploding.

But the drought was too severe, too prolonged. A few grain shipments could not save a civilization. The pleas grew more frantic. A tablet found at Ugarit from a Hittite official reads: "There is famine in our house; we will all die of hunger. If you do not quickly arrive, we will all die of hunger… you will not see a living soul from your country."

The drought was a systemic killer. It struck at the very heart of the palace economy, which was, at its core, an agricultural machine. Without a food surplus, the king had nothing to pay his soldiers, his scribes, his chariot-builders. He could not fund his armies, he could not maintain his temples, he could not control his population. The authority of the god-king evaporated as his subjects starved. The drought did more than cause hunger; it caused a crisis of faith, a loss of confidence in the entire cosmic and political order. The sky had betrayed them, and the king, who was supposed to be the intermediary with the gods, was powerless to stop it.

When the Earth Moved

As if a multi-generational drought were not enough, the Glimmering World was assaulted by a second, even more terrifying force of nature. While the sky burned, the earth itself began to groan and heave.

The Eastern Mediterranean is one of the most seismically active regions on the planet. It is a crumpled, fractured landscape where the great tectonic plates of Africa, Eurasia, and Arabia grind against each other. The North Anatolian Fault, a massive gash that runs across modern-day Turkey, is a sibling to the San Andreas Fault in California, capable of generating devastating earthquakes. For the people of the

Bronze Age, earthquakes were a known and dreaded fact of life. Palaces were periodically destroyed and rebuilt. But what appears to have happened at the end of the 13th century B.C. was something different, a phenomenon that geologists and archaeologists have dubbed an "earthquake storm" or a "seismic swarm."

The theory, championed by the late Stanford geophysicist Amos Nur, suggests that the period saw not just a random series of unrelated earthquakes, but a progressive sequence of major shocks, cascading along the fault systems of the region. Imagine a fault line as a series of locked segments. When one segment ruptures in a major earthquake, it doesn't just release stress in that location; it transfers that stress to the adjacent, still-locked segments, dramatically increasing the likelihood of them rupturing soon after. It's like a row of dominoes, where the fall of one triggers the next in a chain reaction.

The evidence for this seismic storm is not written in texts, but in rubble. Across the entire region, from Greece to the Levant, major archaeological sites show clear evidence of violent destruction consistent with earthquakes, all dating to a narrow window of time between roughly 1225 and 1175 B.C. The pattern is too widespread and too synchronous to be a coincidence.

Let us take a tour of the destruction. At the great citadel of Mycenae, home of the legendary Agamemnon, archaeologists found the famous Cyclopean walls, built of stones weighing many tons, cracked and displaced. Inside the walls, houses were found destroyed, their walls collapsed, with human skeletons crushed beneath the rubble. At nearby Tiryns, another massive fortress, the destruction is even clearer. Entire sections of its colossal walls were thrown down. A man and a woman were found crushed in a collapsed corridor, their remains buried for three millennia until excavators found them.

Across the Aegean, at the legendary site of Troy on the coast of Turkey, the destruction layer known to archaeologists as Troy VIh shows all the classic signs of a powerful earthquake. Its mighty defensive walls are buckled and split, towers have collapsed, and the houses within are ruined.

Further east, on the Syrian coast, the wealthy port of Ugarit shows the same signature of seismic doom. Walls are toppled in a uniform direction, like piano keys knocked over in a single push. Heavy stone lintels are cracked and thrown to the ground. In Cyprus, the great urban centers of Kition and Enkomi were violently destroyed, only to be hastily rebuilt before being destroyed again.

This was not a single, apocalyptic earthquake. It was likely a series of devastating shocks that rolled through the region over a period of several decades. Each one was a localized catastrophe. An earthquake storm was a civilization-killer.

Imagine you are a potter living in the lower town of Tiryns, outside the main citadel walls. It is a normal afternoon. The sun is hot, the air is still. Suddenly, the world dissolves into violence. A low, terrifying roar comes from the deep earth. The ground begins to shake, not with a gentle tremor, but with a convulsive, sickening violence. The walls of your small, mud-brick house flex and then explode inwards. The noise is deafening—the roar of the earth, the crash of collapsing buildings, the high-pitched screams of your neighbors. You are thrown to the ground, the air thick with choking dust.

If you survive the initial shock, your world is still shattered. Your house is a pile of rubble. The roads are blocked by fallen buildings. The complex underground cisterns that supply the citadel with water may be cracked and useless. The harbor facilities, the lifeblood of your city's trade, are a wreck of splintered piers and sunken warehouses. The delicate terracotta pipes of the irrigation channels in the surrounding fields are smashed, ruining the agricultural infrastructure.

Now, imagine that after you have barely begun to clear the rubble and mourn your dead, an aftershock, or another major quake entirely, hits a few years later. And then another. The psychological toll would be immense. The world would no longer feel stable. The gods were clearly angry, the very ground a treacherous enemy. There would be a profound loss of faith in the ability of the king, in his mighty citadel, to offer protection. What good are Cyclopean walls when the earth itself can throw them down?

The Perfect Storm

Drought and earthquakes. Each, on its own, was a terrible crisis. Together, they formed a perfect storm, a devastating one-two punch that broke the back of the Bronze Age world. The two crises fed off each other, creating a feedback loop of catastrophe.

The drought weakened the palace economies from within, creating famine, social unrest, and forcing the kings to deplete their reserves. The centralized, inflexible system, so efficient in times of plenty, had no answer to a prolonged agricultural collapse.

Then, into this weakened, hungry, and fragile world, came

the earthquakes. The seismic storm delivered the physical knockout blow. It shattered the infrastructure—roads, ports, irrigation systems, palaces—that was essential for trade, administration, and food production. It severed the communication lines between the capital and its provinces. A plea for emergency grain might never reach its destination because the roads were impassable or the port destroyed.

Let us return to our farmer. For five years, his crops have been meager, his family hungry. The palace, which once seemed all-powerful, is failing him. His belief in the king and the gods is shaken. Then, an earthquake destroys his village, cracks his fields, and blocks the road to the nearest town.

What does he do? Does he stay and try to rebuild in a parched and unstable land, praying for the generosity of a king who is himself weakened and isolated?

Or does he look at his starving family, at the ruins of his home, at the cracked and barren earth, and make a rational choice? He abandons his land. He packs what little he has onto an oxcart, gathers his family, and joins the growing stream of displaced, desperate people moving along the broken roads. He is no longer a farmer. He is a refugee.

He has heard stories. Stories of lands to the south, like Egypt, where the great river still floods and the grain grows tall. Stories of coastal towns that are rich but poorly defended. He travels with others like himself, a growing band of the dispossessed. They are hungry, they are angry, and they are armed. If they cannot find a new home peacefully, they are prepared to take one by force.

This is the critical link. The non-human actors—the drought and the earthquakes—created the human catastrophe. They did not just weaken the great empires; they uprooted vast populations, setting in motion the mass migrations that would characterize the end of the age. The mysterious raiders and invaders who appear in the Egyptian and Hittite texts were not demons emerging from a void. They were, in many cases, the victims of this perfect storm of natural disasters, transformed by desperation into aggressors.

The Sea Peoples did not cause the collapse of the Bronze Age world. The world was already collapsing. The earth and the sky had already condemned it. The Sea Peoples were simply its inheritors, the scavengers who arrived to pick over the corpse of a civilization that had been felled by forces far beyond its control. The groaning of the earth and the burning of the sky were the opening notes of a funeral dirge. The screams of the dying in the flames of looted cities would soon follow.

6

Rust in the Bronze Machine

From a distance, the great machine of the palace economy appeared flawless. It was a monumental engine of burnished bronze and polished stone, humming with the power of absolute authority. Its gears were the scribes, its fuel was the tribute of a million farmers, and its output was civilization itself: grand temples, glittering treasures, and the terrible, thundering force of the chariot armies. To an outsider, or even to the king at its controls, this machine must have seemed eternal, a perfect expression of cosmic order designed to run forever.

But machines have a hidden vulnerability. They are susceptible to rust. Rust is not a dramatic, external blow. It is a slow, creeping, internal decay. It begins in the unseen joints and hidden gears, a quiet chemical reaction born of inherent weakness and exposure to the elements. For a time, the machine continues to run, its polished exterior hiding the corrosion within. But the rust spreads, weakening the very structure of the metal, until one day, under a stress it was once designed to handle, a critical gear shatters, a piston seizes, and the entire magnificent engine grinds to a catastrophic halt.

The palace economy was just such a machine. Its own design—its rigid centralization, its top-heavy structure, and its profound social inequalities—was its inherent flaw. The climate change and earthquakes we have witnessed were the corrosive elements that exposed this weakness. They created the relentless pressure that would ultimately shatter the gears of the state. Long before the first Sea Peoples' ship beached on the shores of Egypt or the Levant, the great Bronze Machine was rusting from within. The system was losing its most essential lubricant: the consent of the governed. And in the shadows of the failing state, a new and dangerous power was beginning to coalesce—the power of the dispossessed.

The Unwritten Contract

Every society, from a hunter-gatherer band to a modern superpower, operates on a social contract, a set of unwritten rules and mutual obligations that bind its people together. In the Late Bronze Age, the contract was brutally simple. At the top was the king, a figure who was either a living god, like the Pharaoh, or the chosen steward of the gods on earth. Below him was a tiny, privileged sliver of the population: the royal family, high priests, elite warriors, and the scribal bureaucracy that ran the palace. This was the one percent, the residents of the citadel. Below them was everyone else—the ninety-nine percent—the farmers, herders, laborers, potters, and weavers who made up the vast, anonymous base of the pyramid.

The deal was this: the ninety-nine percent would surrender

a huge portion of their labor and its products to the palace. They tilled the king's land, herded his flocks, and gave up the lion's share of their grain, wine, oil, and wool. This was not "tax" in our sense of the word; it was the king's rightful due as the owner of all things. Their individual economic freedom was negligible.

In return, the palace, the one percent, had two primary obligations. First, it provided **security**. The king's army would protect the farmer from foreign invaders and local bandits. The great Cyclopean walls of Mycenae or the fortified garrisons of Egypt were the physical symbols of this promise. Second, and just as important, the palace provided **stability**. Through its vast, centralized storerooms, it acted as a buffer against scarcity. In a good year, the palace collected a massive surplus. In a bad year, a year of meager harvest, the palace was supposed to open its silos and distribute rations, ensuring that no one starved. It was a system of institutionalized insurance, a guarantee against the caprices of nature.

For centuries, this contract, though starkly unequal, held. The farmer might resent the wealth of the palace, but he depended on its protection and its stored grain. His life was hard, but it was predictable. The king's legitimacy, his divine right to rule, was inextricably tied to his ability to uphold his end of this bargain. The system worked, as long as the harvests were good and the enemies were conventional. But what would happen if the palace could no longer keep its promises? What happened when the rust set in?

The Great Squeeze: A Three-Year Catastrophe

Let us return to the drought, the great catalyst of the collapse. We can model its effect on the palace machine not as a single event, but as a slow, agonizing process of systemic starvation.

Year One of the Drought: The harvest is poor, perhaps only sixty percent of the normal yield. Across the kingdom, farmers look to the sky with anxiety, but their immediate fear is blunted by the promise of the palace. At the capital, the scribes make their calculations. The tribute collected is far below projections. But the king is not yet worried. This is precisely what the surplus is for. He issues the command, and the great stone and mud-brick silos are opened. Rations are distributed as normal. The textile workers, the potters, the bronze smiths, the soldiers—all receive their allotted measures of barley and oil. The social contract holds. The machine, though drawing on its reserves, is still running smoothly. The king's power is affirmed.

Year Two of the Drought: The rains fail again. This time, the harvest is a disaster, less than half the normal yield. A genuine panic begins to ripple through the countryside. At the palace, the scribes' new calculations are terrifying. The tribute collected is a pittance, and the great surplus from previous years is now gone. The king is faced with impossible choices. There is not enough food to go around.

Who gets fed? The logic of power is ruthless. The king must preserve the core instruments of his rule. The elite *maryannu* warriors, the chariot drivers who form the backbone of his army, receive their full rations. The high-ranking scribes and priests, the men who run the administration and placate the gods, are protected. The king's own extensive household, with its hundreds of courtiers, servants, and concubines, continues to feast.

But someone must pay the price. The rations for the female weavers in the palace workshops are cut in half. The laborers conscripted to build a new temple extension are sent home with empty hands. And in the rural villages, the local overseers are instructed to collect the king's tribute as usual, even if it leaves the farmers with nothing but seed corn for the next, increasingly hopeless, planting season.

This is the moment the rust becomes visible. A chasm opens up between the gilded, well-fed elite of the citadel and the hungry, struggling populace. The farmer, who sees the royal steward carry away his last sacks of grain, knows that the king and his court are not sharing in his suffering. He sees the promise of stability for the cruel fiction it is. The social contract has been broken, not by him, but by the palace. Resentment, the most corrosive of social acids, begins to eat away at the bonds of loyalty.

Year Three of the Drought: Catastrophe. The harvest is non-existent. The fields are dust. The great silos of the palace are cavernous and empty. The king is now powerless. He can no longer feed even his own soldiers, let alone the general population. The machine has run out of fuel. The system has completely failed.

The farmer in his village now faces a stark choice. He can stay on his ancestral land and watch his children starve. He can appeal to the gods, who seem to have abandoned him. Or he can abandon the system that has abandoned him. He can walk away from his land, his village, his king. He can take his family, his axe, and his desperation, and become something new. He can become an outlaw. He can become one of the *Habiru*.

The Rise of the Habiru: A Social Disease

The term appears again and again in the texts of the Late Bronze Age, a constant source of anxiety for the established powers. In Akkadian, they are the *'Apiru*. In Egyptian, the *'pr.w*. In the desperate letters of Rib-Hadda of Byblos, they are a shadowy menace, overrunning his lands and luring away his people. For a long time, scholars, noting the similarity of the word, believed the Habiru were the ancient Hebrews of the Old Testament. While there may be a distant linguistic and social connection, the truth is far broader and more significant.

The Habiru were not an ethnic group. They were not a nation. They were a social phenomenon, a class of people defined by what they were not. They were stateless, landless, lawless. They were people who existed outside the neat, ordered structure of the palace economy. They were runaway slaves, political refugees, draft dodgers, failed farmers, and opportunistic bandits. They were the dropouts, the outcasts, the human debris of a disintegrating society. They were, in short, a symptom of the rust, the human personification of the system's failure.

In times of stability, the Habiru were a manageable problem, a fringe element living in the hills and deserts, occasionally raiding a caravan. But in the crisis of the late 13th century B.C., their numbers swelled. The failing palace economies began to hemorrhage people, and these desperate souls found a new home in the growing bands of the Habiru.

The Amarna letters give us a vivid picture of their destabilizing effect. Rib-Hadda of Byblos complains constantly that his rival, Abdi-Ashirta, is a "dog" who has joined with the Habiru. He writes to the Pharaoh: "The Habiru are stronger than I… The sons of Abdi-Ashirta and the Habiru are seizing the king's lands for themselves… The land is the Habiru's land!" He paints a picture of a countryside in chaos, where the authority of the palace has evaporated, replaced by the authority of outlaw warlords and their Habiru armies. He even reports that his own farmers are deserting him to join their ranks. The choice was simple: starve loyally with Rib-Hadda, or eat with the outlaws.

The Habiru created a vicious feedback loop of collapse. As the drought and palace failures created more Habiru, the Habiru themselves accelerated the system's decay. They raided the farms that were still producing, stealing the very grain that was supposed to go to the palace storerooms. They ambushed merchant caravans, severing the trade routes that brought essential goods like tin and copper to the capital. They created a landscape of fear and insecurity, making it impossible for the palace to project its authority.

For a peasant on the edge of starvation, the Habiru offered a powerful alternative. They offered freedom from the crushing burden of tribute. They offered community with others who shared their plight. And most of all, they offered agency. As a Habiru, you were no longer a passive victim of fate; you were a raider, a mercenary, a survivor who took what you needed by force. They became a parallel society, a shadow kingdom growing in the ruins of the old order.

Walls of Fear and Tombs of Gold

How did the elite, huddled within their palace walls, respond to this growing internal chaos? The archaeological record suggests a twofold response: fear and denial.

The fear is visible in stone. Across Greece, in the final decades before their destruction, the Mycenaean palaces engaged in a frenzy of defensive construction. The walls of Mycenae, Tiryns, and Athens were massively expanded and strengthened. But most tellingly, these new fortifications often included protecting the water supply. At both Mycenae and Tiryns, elaborate secret passages were built, leading from inside the citadel down to hidden underground cisterns.

Why was this so important? An external army would bring its own water. But a besieged citadel faces two threats: the enemy outside the walls, and the thirsty, desperate population of the lower town that has fled inside for protection. These secret water sources were a defense against a long siege, but the

7

Whispers from the West

History rarely announces its turning points with a thunderclap.

More often, the great transformations begin as whispers, as faint, unsettling tremors on the periphery of the known world. While the Great Kings of Egypt and Hatti were preoccupied with their grand rivalries, their famines, and the growing rust in their own imperial machines, a new kind of story began to circulate in the port cities and military outposts of their empires. These were not tales of rival kings or rebellious vassals—the familiar antagonists of their world. These were stories of something new, something unpredictable, coming from the sea.

They were whispers of ghost fleets and pirate dens, of coastal towns pillaged in the night, and of strange, warlike peoples with unfamiliar names and unsettling customs. For decades, even for generations, before the final, cataclysmic wave of invasions, these whispers grew in volume and intensity. They were the early warning signs of the coming storm, the advance scouts of a new and more chaotic age.

These early raiders were the first of the peoples who would later be lumped together under the generic and terrifying Egyptian label, "the Sea Peoples." But in these early days, they were not a unified confederation. They were disparate groups, opportunistic pirates, and skilled mercenaries, probing the edges of the great empires, testing their defenses, and discovering, to their own surprise, that the colossal structures of the Bronze Age were perhaps not as strong as they appeared. They were both a cause and a symptom of the growing instability, a new breed of predator thriving in the increasingly turbulent waters of a changing world. To understand the final collapse, we must first listen to these whispers and trace the origins of the mystery villains who were slowly, inexorably, sailing out of the West.

The Wild West of the Bronze Age

Our story begins not with a grand invasion, but with a geographical problem. To the east and south of the great empires lay established kingdoms and well-trodden trade routes. To the north lay the Black Sea, a world unto itself. But to the west, beyond the well-traveled sea lanes connecting Crete and the Greek mainland, lay a region that was, to the scribes of Egypt and Hatti, a kind of "Wild West." This was western Anatolia, the rugged, fractured coastline of modern-day Turkey, a patchwork of small, fiercely independent kingdoms that had always resisted easy categorization and control.

This was the land of Arzawa, of the Seha River Land, and, most notoriously, the Lukka Lands. The Lukka were the perennial troublemakers of the Bronze Age, the wild card in the deck of international politics. The Hittite kings were in a state of almost constant frustration with them. They were not a single, unified kingdom that could be defeated in battle and forced to sign a treaty. They were a loose confederation of highland clans and coastal communities, pirates by inclination and warriors by trade. They were a people who lived in the cracks of the imperial system.

Hittite texts are filled with exasperated references to the Lukka. One moment, a Lukka chieftain might be a loyal vassal of the Hittite king; the next, he might be sacking a neighboring pro-Hittite city or hiring out his warriors to the king's enemies. They were slippery, opportunistic, and utterly unreliable. A treaty signed with one Lukka town meant nothing to the town in the next valley. They were a constant, low-level irritant, a source of instability that the Hittite empire could never quite stamp out.

And their primary sphere of operation was the sea. The Lukka were infamous pirates. They knew the rugged coastline, with its hidden coves and secret anchorages, better than anyone. From these lairs, they would launch raids on the rich merchant ships that plied the coastal routes, the arteries of the globalized economy. A letter from the king of Cyprus (Alashiya) to the Pharaoh Akhenaten, found in the Amarna archives, complains bitterly about them. "Men of the Lukka," the Cypriot king writes, "year after year, seize my villages." He protests his innocence, claiming they are not his people, but he cannot control them. They are a law unto themselves.

For centuries, the Lukka were a manageable threat. Their piracy was a cost of doing business, a background noise in the hum of international trade. A wise captain paid for an armed escort or traveled in a convoy. But as the 13th century B.C. progressed, as the drought bit deeper and the central authority of the Hittite empire began to weaken, the Lukka problem escalated. Their raids grew bolder, more frequent, more destructive. They were no longer just a nuisance; they were a genuine threat to the economic lifeline of the great powers. They were a sign that the old order, which had kept such chaos largely in check, was beginning to lose its grip. The police were losing control of the bad neighborhoods.

The Mercenary with the Horned Helmet

The growing chaos at sea created not just predators, but also opportunities. In an increasingly violent world, the demand for skilled fighting men skyrocketed. And if a king could not rely on the loyalty of his own starving soldiers, he might look elsewhere, hiring professionals whose only allegiance was to their paymaster. This was the age of the mercenary, and a new group of seafaring warriors from the West soon emerged as the most sought-after and formidable soldiers-for-hire on the market: the Sherden.

The Sherden are one of the most fascinating and enigmatic of all the Sea Peoples. Their name first appears in the Amarna letters, where they are mentioned as raiders and as members of the Pharaoh's own garrison in Byblos. But they burst onto the main stage during the reign of Ramesses II, the great victor—or propagandist—of Kadesh.

In the second year of his reign, long before his Syrian campaign, Ramesses faced a major threat from the sea. An inscription from Tanis records the event: "The Sherden of the rebellious heart, whom none have ever known how to combat, they came boldly in their warships from the midst of the sea, none being able to stand before them."

This is a classic piece of pharaonic hyperbole, but the core of the story is clear. A fleet of Sherden warships launched a direct, audacious raid on the Egyptian Delta. Ramesses claims to have trapped and defeated them, capturing many as prisoners. But what happened next is the truly remarkable part of the story. Ramesses did not simply execute or enslave these defeated enemies. He recognized their extraordinary fighting prowess and did something utterly pragmatic: he incorporated them into his own army.

From that moment on, the Sherden became a permanent and highly visible part of the Egyptian military machine. They became the elite shock troops, the special forces of the Pharaoh. In the famous reliefs of the Battle of Kadesh, they are instantly recognizable. They are depicted fighting fiercely for Ramesses, distinguished by their unique and terrifying battle-gear. They carry large, round shields—a stark contrast to the rectangular shields of the Egyptians. They wield long, straight, slashing swords, a weapon type unfamiliar to the Egyptians who favored the sickle-like *khepesh*. And most distinctively, they wear magnificent helmets, each adorned with a pair of sharp, forward-curving horns, with a solar disk or a spike rising from the center. They look like Vikings who have sailed into the wrong millennium.

The presence of the Sherden in the Pharaoh's own body-guard is a stunning testament to the changing nature of the world. The Glimmering World of the Great Club had been an insular, aristocratic system. A king's power was demonstrated by his native-born *maryannu* warriors. The hiring of foreign mercenaries was once seen as a sign of weakness. But by the time of Ramesses II, it had become a necessity. The world was more violent, the old rules were eroding, and a king needed the best fighters he could get, regardless of their origin.

But who *were* the Sherden? Their origin is one of the great unsolved mysteries of the Bronze Age. Their distinctive helmets and swords have no clear parallels in the Levant or Egypt. The closest matches are found far to the west, in the material culture of Sardinia and among the Nuragic civilization that flourished there. The name "Sherden" is tantalizingly close to "Sardinia." Is it possible that these sea warriors originated from this distant western island? Or did they perhaps settle there *after* the period of the collapse, bringing their culture with them?

The debate rages on, but the most likely scenario is that the Sherden, like the Lukka, were a product of the growing instability in the Central and Eastern Mediterranean. They may have been displaced peoples, victims of the same climate-driven famines and social upheavals that were beginning to afflict the entire region. They took to the sea, using their martial skills to survive, first as pirates, then as mercenaries for the richest employer they could find.

Their story reveals the deep paradox at the heart of the Late Bronze Age system in its final decades. The Pharaoh of Egypt, the most powerful man in the world, was using foreign mercenaries to defend his empire from... other foreign raiders, some of whom were likely the Sherdens' own kinsmen. The system was becoming a snake eating its own tail. The lines between insider and outsider, friend and foe, were becoming dangerously blurred. The Pharaoh had hired the wolves to guard the sheepfold, a pragmatic solution that underscored the terrifying fact that the wolves were now everywhere.

The First Great Wave: The Libyan War of Merneptah

For decades, the whispers remained on the periphery. The Lukka raided, the Sherden served, and the great empires continued their slow, grand decline. Then, in the late 13th century B.C., the whispers became a roar. The disparate threats that had been probing the edges of the system coalesced into a major, coordinated assault. This was not yet the final invasion that would be faced by Ramesses III, but it was its dress rehearsal, a terrifying preview of the new way of war.

The crisis fell upon Egypt during the reign of the Pharaoh Merneptah, the elderly son and successor of Ramesses the Great. Around 1208 B.C., in the fifth year of his reign, Merneptah faced an invasion that was unlike any Egypt had seen before. The attack came from the west, from Libya. The Libyans had always been troublesome neighbors, periodically raiding the fertile lands of the western Delta. But this was different.

The Libyan leader, a chief named Meryey, had forged a grand coalition. He had unified the Libyan tribes and, crucially, had allied himself with a host of seafaring peoples from the north. A great victory inscription of Merneptha, known as the Great Karnak Inscription, lists these new allies by name, and it reads like a chilling roll call of the coming apocalypse:

"The wretched chief of Libya... has fallen upon the country of Tehenu with his archers... Shekelesh, Ekwesh, Teresh of the countries of the sea, Lukka... taking the best of every warrior and every man of war of his country."

Here, for the first time, we see the familiar names of the Lukka and the Sherden joined by a new cast of characters: the Shekelesh, the Teresh, and the Ekwesh. These were all peoples "of the countries of the sea." This was a formal alliance between a land-based power and a coalition of sea-raiders. Their goal was not just plunder, but settlement. The inscription is explicit on this point. The invaders came with their families and their cattle, "to seek sustenance for their bodies."

This is a critical moment. The pattern we saw hinted at in the story of the Habiru and the early raiders has now burst into the open. The drought, famine, and social collapse in the lands to the north and west of Egypt were now driving whole populations to migrate, and they were doing so as an armed, organized military force. They were not just raiding for loot; they were fighting for a new home, a place to settle in the rich, well-watered lands of Egypt.

The Ekwesh are a particularly interesting case. The Egyptian text notes, uniquely, that they were "of the countries of the sea, who had no foreskins"—in other words, they were uncircumcised. This detail, combined with the similarity of the name, has led many scholars to identify the Ekwesh with the *Achaeans*—the very same name Homer used for the Mycenaean Greeks. Is it possible that groups of Mycenaeans, their own palaces beginning to crumble under the weight of drought and earthquake, had taken to the sea as mercenaries and migrants, joining a Libyan warlord in a desperate bid to conquer a piece of the Nile Delta?

The invasion was a massive threat. The combined force penetrated deep into Egyptian territory. Merneptah's inscription describes the terror of the Egyptian populace: "The forts of the western frontier were abandoned, the wells were stopped up… their fields were left to the cattle." But Merneptah, though old, was a seasoned commander. He mustered his army, including his own loyal Sherden mercenaries, and met the invaders in a great battle near the town of Perire.

After a six-hour battle, the Egyptians were victorious. The inscription crows over the result, giving precise, if likely exaggerated, numbers of the slain: over 6,000 Libyans and their allies killed, and more than 9,000 taken prisoner. Meryey, the Libyan chief, is said to have abandoned his bow, his quiver, and his sandals, and fled into the night.

Merneptah had saved Egypt. He celebrated his victory with a series of inscriptions, including the famous "Israel Stele," so-named because it contains the first known extra-biblical reference to a people called Israel in Canaan. But his victory hymn has a dark, ominous undertone. He boasts of his triumph, but the tone is one of profound relief, the sigh of a man who has stared into the abyss. He had defeated a massive, migrating horde, a new kind of enemy whose desperation made them incredibly dangerous.

And he knew they were not the only ones. The victory had been won, the wave had been repulsed, but the sea from which it came was still churning. The victory of Merneptah was not an end to the problem. It was a temporary reprieve. It was a successful test of Egypt's defenses, but it also revealed the terrifying scale of the forces that were now in motion across the Mediterranean. The whispers from the West had become a full-throated war cry.

The Hittite Collapse: A Silent Scream

While Egypt was successfully repelling this first great wave, its old rival, the Hittite Empire, was facing its own existential crisis. And unlike the Egyptians, they would not survive. The end of the Hittite Empire is one of the most sudden and complete societal collapses in human history. A superpower that had dominated Anatolia for four hundred years simply vanishes from the historical record.

There is no great inscription from the last Hittite king detailing his final, heroic battle. There is no epic poem. The end of Hatti is a silent scream, a story we must piece together from the burned ruins of its capital and the desperate, final letters found in the archives of its vassals.

The same forces that were driving raiders towards Egypt were tearing the Hittite Empire apart from within and without. The megadrought had crippled its agricultural heartland, leading to the desperate pleas for grain we have already seen. The ceaseless problem of the Lukka pirates and other Anatolian rebels grew from a nuisance into a fatal cancer, disrupting trade and communication. The final Hittite king, Šuppiluliuma II, seems to have spent his entire reign fighting a desperate, multi-front war to hold his fragmenting empire together.

An inscription from his reign records a series of naval battles off the coast of Cyprus against the ships of Alashiya. This is a shocking development. Cyprus, the copper-rich island, had been a key trading partner and sometime vassal of the Hittites for centuries. Now, the Hittites were fighting a sea war against them. Why? Had the Cypriot king thrown his lot in with the sea raiders? Or was this a desperate Hittite attempt to seize the island's resources by force in a last-ditch effort to save their collapsing economy?

Whatever the cause, the campaign seems to have been a pyrrhic victory at best. The Hittite king, focused on this naval war to the south, was distracted from the rot that was consuming his Anatolian heartland.

The final, tantalizing clues come from the archives of Ugarit, the rich port city on the Syrian coast. A letter from the king of Ugarit, Ammurapi, replies to a desperate request for aid from the king of Alashiya (Cyprus). Ammurapi's reply is chilling: "My father, behold, the enemy's ships came (here); my cities were burned, and they did evil things in my country... Does not my father know that all my troops and chariots are in the land of Hatti, and all my ships are in the land of Lukka? ...Thus, the country is abandoned to itself."

This is an astonishing snapshot of the final, chaotic days. The king of Ugarit has sent his entire army inland to help his Hittite overlord fight some unknown enemy, while his entire fleet is away on patrol, fighting the Lukka pirates. And at this very moment of maximum vulnerability, a new, unnamed enemy fleet appears and begins to burn his cities. The carefully balanced system of alliances and mutual defense had completely broken down into a frantic, every-man-for-himself scramble for survival.

Soon after this letter was written, the great capital of Hattusa was violently destroyed and abandoned, never to be reoccupied. The mighty Hittite Empire, the great rival of Egypt, the other pillar of the Bronze Age world, was gone.

Who delivered the final blow? Was it the Kaska tribes from the north? Internal rebels? Famine? Or was it the Sea

Peoples? The answer is likely all of the above. The empire was a hollowed-out shell, rotten from within by famine and revolt, and battered from without by constant warfare. The final push could have come from any direction.

The fall of the Hittites created a massive power vacuum. It removed the northern bulwark that had, however imperfectly, helped to contain the chaos in Anatolia and the Aegean. It was like a dam bursting. The pressures that had been building in the West were now free to surge eastward and southward, in a great, unimpeded wave.

The whispers had now reached a crescendo. The early tremors had given way to a world-shaking earthquake. The disparate groups of pirates, mercenaries, and migrants—the Lukka, the Sherden, the Ekwesh, the Shekelesh—were about to be joined by others, all displaced by the same perfect storm of climate, earthquake, and collapse. They were coalescing into the great, final confederation that would bear down on the last remaining powers of the Levant and Egypt. The dress rehearsal was over. The main event was about to begin.

III

The Great Unraveling

The whispers have become a scream. The tremors have become a world-breaking earthquake. The scattered bands of raiders and refugees, forged in the crucible of drought and famine, now coalesce into a great, unstoppable wave. The time for warnings is over. The Great Unraveling has begun.

8

The Last Letter from Ugarit

History is an ocean of silence, and what we know of the past are merely the small, scattered islands of evidence that have survived the tide of time. Most of the Bronze Age world vanished without a sound. The great Hittite Empire fell with a silent scream. The glittering palaces of Mycenaean Greece collapsed into a voiceless ruin, their stories fading into myth. But in one place, on the sun-drenched coast of Syria, the silence was broken. In one place, the final, frantic heartbeats of a dying city were preserved, its last words captured for eternity. That place was the kingdom of Ugarit.

The story of Ugarit's destruction is not one we have to reconstruct from silent rubble or the boastful propaganda of a distant king. It is a story told by the city's own inhabitants, in their own words. Because of a series of archaeological miracles—a forgotten archive, a desperate scribe, and a final, all-consuming fire—we have the last letters from Ugarit. We have the incoming and outgoing correspondence of the city's final days, a real-time account of a civilization watching its own doom sail in from the sea.

To read these tablets is to experience the collapse not as an abstract historical process, but as a deeply personal and human tragedy. It is to feel the rising panic of officials left to defend a city stripped of its army, to hear the desperate pleas for help, and to witness the agonizing, slow-motion wreck of a rich, cosmopolitan world. The fall of Ugarit is perhaps the most poignant and best-documented moment of the entire Bronze Age Collapse. It is a dispatch from the edge of the abyss, a final letter, sent but never delivered, from a world that was about to disappear forever.

The Jewel of the Levant

Before we can witness its fall, we must appreciate the jewel that was Ugarit. Situated on the Mediterranean coast at the magnificent bay of Ras Shamra, Ugarit was the quintessential Bronze Age success story. For centuries, it had thrived by being the perfect middleman. It was the crucial gateway, the logistical and commercial hub that connected the maritime world of the Mediterranean with the great land-based empires of Mesopotamia and Anatolia. It was here that the tin from Afghanistan, carried overland on dusty caravan trails, was loaded onto ships bound for Crete. It was here that the fine linen and papyrus of Egypt were exchanged for the timber and olive oil of the Levant.

As we have seen, the city was a vibrant, multicultural metropolis. Its archives were written in eight different languages and five different scripts. Its streets would have thronged with a diverse cast of characters: Mycenaean merchants in their fine woolen tunics, Hittite officials in their pointed shoes, Egyptian envoys in their stark white kilts, and Babylonian traders with their long, curled beards, all haggling in the lingua franca of Akkadian. The wealth generated by this trade was immense. The palace of Ugarit was a sprawling, luxurious complex of ninety rooms, multiple courtyards, and its own lush, walled garden. The grand villas of the city's merchant princes were two-story affairs with private family tombs, sophisticated plumbing, and archives filled with international business contracts.

Ugarit's greatest innovation, born of its fast-paced commercial culture, was the alphabet. The scribes of Ugarit, finding the complex syllabic cuneiform of Mesopotamia too cumbersome for their needs, developed a revolutionary streamlined script of just thirty signs, each representing a single consonant. This was a quantum leap in information technology, a democratization of writing that would ultimately, through its Phoenician descendants, give birth to the Greek, Roman, and modern alphabets we use today. This was a city of incredible sophistication, a beacon of literacy, wealth, and culture.

But Ugarit's success was also its vulnerability. It was a vassal state, caught in the gravitational pull of the Hittite Empire to the north. As a loyal subject of the Great King of Hatti, the king of Ugarit was bound by treaty to provide troops and ships in times of war. Its wealth was a magnet for pirates, its coastal location a source of constant exposure. Its prosperity depended entirely on the stability of the international system, the very system that was now unraveling with terrifying speed. Ugarit was a beautiful ship, moored in what had once been a safe harbor, but the sea was growing rough, and the great imperial anchor that had held it steady was beginning to drag.

The Last King of Ugarit

Our story centers on the city's last known ruler, a man named Ammurapi. He was a young king, likely ascending to the throne around 1215 B.C. He inherited a kingdom facing a perfect storm of crises. The drought that was devastating the Hittite heartland was also affecting the Levant, leading to food shortages and social unrest. The ever-present threat of sea raiders was growing more acute. And his Hittite overlord, Šuppiluliuma II, was engaged in a desperate, all-consuming struggle to hold his own fragmenting empire together, demanding ever more resources from his loyal vassals.

Ammurapi found himself trapped. His primary duty was to his own kingdom, but his treaty obligations to the Hittites were absolute. A series of letters found in the Ugaritic archives reveal the immense pressure he was under. The Hittite court sent a stream of increasingly strident demands for tribute, for troops, and, most urgently, for grain. One letter from a high-ranking Hittite official is a thinly veiled threat, chastising the young king for being slow to send a promised shipment of food.

Faced with this relentless pressure from his overlord and the growing instability at sea, Ammurapi made a fateful, though perhaps unavoidable, decision. He honored his treaty obligations. He sent the bulk of the Ugaritic army, including its vital chariot corps, inland to assist the Hittite king in his campaigns in Anatolia. At the same time, he dispatched the entire Ugaritic fleet to patrol the western coast of Anatolia, hunting for the Lukka pirates who were disrupting the sea lanes.

In doing so, he stripped his own kingdom of its defenses. The jewel of the Levant, one of the richest cities in the world, was left naked and exposed, its walls guarded by a skeleton crew, its harbor empty of warships. The king himself may have been away with his troops. The stage was set for a tragedy.

The Kiln

The final act of Ugarit's drama was discovered not in the grand throne room of the palace, but in a small, unassuming workshop. It was a kiln, a simple oven used for baking clay tablets. In the normal course of events, an archive was a living thing. Scribes would create temporary records on wet clay—inventories, receipts, short-term contracts. Once the information was no longer needed, or had been transferred to a more permanent summary document, the tablets would be recycled, their clay moistened and smoothed for reuse. Only the most important documents—treaties, royal decrees, literary texts—were deliberately fired in a kiln to make them permanent.

In the final days of Ugarit, it appears a scribe, or a group of scribes, made a desperate decision. They gathered up a collection of the most recent and urgent diplomatic correspondence—the letters that had just arrived, the draft replies that were waiting to be sent—and placed them in the kiln. Perhaps they were trying to create a permanent record of the crisis for the king upon his return. Perhaps, in a moment of pure chaos, they were simply trying to save the most vital intelligence their city possessed. They lit the fire.

They never had the chance to take the tablets out. The city fell. The workshop was destroyed, and the kiln was buried. And in that earthen oven, the last words of Ugarit were preserved, fired hard as rock by the very disaster they documented. The fires of the city's destruction ironically immortalized its death throes. When French archaeologists unearthed this kiln in 1952, they found a time capsule of terror, a collection of tablets that allow us to reconstruct the city's final days, almost hour by hour.

Let us imagine that scribe. Let's call him Urtenu, the name of a real high official whose archives were found in a grand villa near the palace. The city is in a state of high alert. Refugees are streaming in from the coastal villages, their faces masks of terror, telling wild stories of strange ships and burned fields. The smoke from distant fires can be seen smudging the pristine blue horizon. The harbor is eerily empty, the great fleet away on the king's business. The army is gone. Fear, thick and suffocating, hangs over the city like the dust of the drought.

Urtenu knows the situation is critical. He has just received a series of frantic messages. A rider, his horse lathered in sweat, has arrived from the north with a tablet from a neighboring king. A merchant ship, having narrowly escaped the enemy, has brought a letter from Cyprus. His own scouts have returned with terrifying reports. He understands that this is a crisis unlike any other. This information must be preserved.

He gathers the tablets, his hands trembling slightly. These

are not grand literary works. They are hastily written notes, pleas, warnings. He carries them from the main archive to the small kiln in the scribal workshop. As he carefully places them on the shelf inside the oven, he can hear shouts from the city walls. A watchman's horn blows, not a call to arms, but a long, mournful wail of despair. He knows there is no time. He orders the fire to be lit, the heat beginning to rise, the clay beginning its slow transformation into stone. He is trying to save his city's memory, even as the city itself is dying around him.

A Cascade of Warnings

Let us now open the kiln and read the last letters from Ugarit. They are a cascade of warnings, a chorus of panic from across the Eastern Mediterranean, all converging on this single, doomed city.

One of the most powerful letters (RS 18.147) is from the Great King of the Hittites himself, Šuppiluliuma II. It is a reply to an earlier, now-lost, letter from Ammurapi, in which the young king had apparently expressed his fear of an impending naval attack. The Hittite king's reply is a classic example of an overlord completely misreading the scale of the threat. He is dismissive, almost scolding.

"As for what you have written to me," Šuppiluliuma writes, "'Ships of the enemy have been seen at sea!'—even if it is true, remain firm. But in fact, be very firm! What is your fear? ... Surround your city with walls. Bring your infantry and chariots inside. And wait for the enemy with a firm foot."

It is the advice of a man whose entire military experience is based on land warfare. He sees the enemy as a conventional army that will lay siege to a city. He does not grasp the new reality of lightning-fast naval raids. And his advice is tragically useless. Ammurapi *cannot* bring his infantry and chariots inside the city, because they are hundreds of miles away, fighting the king's own battles in Anatolia. The letter is a testament to the fatal disconnect between the imperial center and its vulnerable periphery. The Great King, fighting for his own life, is blind to the imminent destruction of his most valuable vassal.

Another letter (RS 20.238), this one from a high-ranking official or king of Cyprus (Alashiya), is even more terrifying. It is a direct warning about the enemy fleet that is now at sea.

"My father," the letter begins, a term of respect between rulers, "the enemy ships are here! They have set fire to my towns and have done evil things to my country. Does not my father know this? All my troops and chariots are in the land of Hatti, and all my ships are in the land of Lukka... My father, be aware of this!"

This is the letter we saw briefly in the last chapter, but its context here is devastating. The king of Ugarit has just received this message. An allied kingdom is being burned by the same enemy fleet that is, at this very moment, sailing towards his own defenseless coast. And his situation is identical to that of the Cypriot king: his army is in Hatti, his fleet is in the Lukka lands. The two kingdoms, stripped of their defenses by their obligations to their Hittite overlord, are being picked off one by one. The letter is not a request for help; it is a scream of shared, helpless terror.

The identity of this enemy is never explicitly stated. They are simply "the enemy," a faceless, implacable force. But another tablet from the kiln (RS 34.129) gives us a clue. It is a letter from a man named Eshuwara, the grand vizier of Cyprus. He writes to the king of Ugarit to inform him that he has been questioned by the king of Hatti about a group known as the *Shikila*. Eshuwara says, "The Shikila... who live on ships, they have captured the towns in your country."

The Shikila. This is almost certainly the *Shekelesh*, one of the peoples named in both Merneptah's and Ramesses III's great inscriptions as key members of the Sea Peoples confederation. Here, we have a direct, contemporary link. The mysterious enemy from the sea is not a ghost. It has a name. And it is systematically destroying the coastal cities of the Levant.

The Final Moments

With these warnings in hand, the officials left in charge of Ugarit could only watch and wait. The city's fate was sealed. The final tablets from the kiln paint a picture of the city's last, desperate hours.

One tablet (RS L 1) appears to be a report from a scout sent to observe the enemy's advance. The writing is hurried, the message stark: "To my lord, say: The enemy's ships are seven. They have done harm." Just seven ships. This was not a massive invasion fleet in the style of the Persian Wars. This was a lightning raid, a targeted strike by a small, agile force against a city they knew to be defenseless. This was the new face of war: fast, brutal, and asymmetrical.

The most poignant tablet of all (RS 20.18) is a letter from

King Ammurapi himself, likely a draft of a message he intended to send to the king of Cyprus, a reply to the desperate warning he had received. It is a letter that was never sent. It is the voice of a young king watching his world burn down around him.

"My father, now the ships of the enemy have come. They have burned my cities with fire and have done evil deeds in my country. My father does not know that all my troops are stationed in the land of Hatti and all my ships are in the land of Lukka? They have not yet reached me. The land is thus abandoned to itself. May my father know this. The seven ships of the enemy that have come have inflicted great damage upon us."

It is a recitation of utter helplessness. He can only repeat the terrible facts: the enemy is here, my army is gone, my fleet is gone, I am alone. The phrase "the land is abandoned to itself" is a summary of the entire collapse. The imperial systems, the alliances, the treaties—all of it had failed. In the final analysis, every king, every city, was on its own.

Sometime around 1185 B.C., the enemy arrived at Ugarit. There was no great siege, no pitched battle. The archaeological evidence points to a sudden, violent, and total destruction. A thick layer of ash and rubble covers the entire site. In the grand palace and the wealthy villas, archaeologists found treasures left where they fell—a solid gold bowl, a carved ivory pyxis shaped like a goddess—a sign that the inhabitants fled or were killed with no time to gather their valuables. Skeletons were found in the rubble of collapsed houses. A bronze hoard was discovered hidden in a well, a treasure its owner never had the chance to retrieve.

The city of Ugarit, the jewel of the Levant, a center of commerce and culture for half a millennium, was extinguished in a single day of fire and slaughter. Its smoke was a funeral pyre for an entire way of life.

The Aftermath: A World in Ruins

The fall of Ugarit was not an isolated event. It was a key domino in a cascade of destruction that swept across the Eastern Mediterranean. The same destruction layer, dating to this same narrow window of time, is found at city after city up and down the Levantine coast. Alalakh, Tell Sukas, Kadesh—all burned. Further south, the great Canaanite cities of Lachish and Megiddo were violently destroyed. The entire urban landscape of the Bronze Age Levant was wiped from the map.

What happened to the people? Some were killed. Some were taken as slaves. But many, it seems, joined the wave. The destruction of cities like Ugarit did not stop the migration; it fed it. The survivors, their homes destroyed, their livelihoods gone, had no choice but to join the very people who had uprooted them. The great wave of the Sea Peoples was like a tsunami, not only destroying the coastline but also pulling the debris and the survivors back into its own churning mass.

The destruction of Ugarit was a catastrophe not just for its inhabitants, but for the entire Glimmering World. It was the severing of a primary artery. The great crossroads of international trade was now a smoking ruin. The flow of goods and ideas between the sea and the land, between east and west, was halted. The intricate web of commerce that had sustained the Bronze Age world was irrevocably torn.

The last letters from the kiln of Ugarit are therefore more than just a local tragedy. They are a universal testament to the fragility of complex societies. They show how a world built on interdependence can be terrifyingly vulnerable to systemic shocks. They reveal how quickly the institutions of power—alliances, treaties, armies—can evaporate in the face of a novel threat.

The image of the scribe Urtenu, frantically trying to preserve his city's final moments, is an icon of the end of an age. He was a man of a system, a creature of the palace, a believer in the power of the written word to create order out of chaos. His world was one of lists, contracts, and carefully worded diplomatic correspondence. In the end, all he could do was document the arrival of a new world, a world that had no use for his treaties or his lists, a world that communicated not with the stylus, but with the torch. His last, desperate act of preservation, a final flicker of the civilized mind against the encroaching darkness, is the enduring legacy of the city he could not save.

9

The End of the Heroes

Long after the Bronze Age had collapsed into dust and memory, when the art of writing had been forgotten and the great citadels were the vine-choked ruins of a half-remembered past, a blind poet sang of heroes. He sang of Agamemnon, "lord of men," who marshaled a thousand ships to sail against Troy. He sang of wise Nestor of Pylos, of mighty Achilles, and of cunning Odysseus. The poet, whom we call Homer, was singing of a lost world, a glorious, bygone era of god-like kings, bronze-clad warriors, and epic deeds. For centuries, his stories, the *Iliad* and the *Odyssey*, were thought to be just that: magnificent fictions, foundational myths from the dawn of Greek civilization.

Then, in the 19th century, a brash and obsessive German businessman named Heinrich Schliemann, armed with a shovel in one hand and a copy of Homer in the other, set out to prove that this world was real. His spectacular, if often clumsy, excavations at Troy and Mycenae uncovered a lost civilization of immense wealth and power. He found golden death masks, bronze daggers inlaid with scenes of lion hunts, and walls built of stones so large they seemed the work of giants. This was the world of the Mycenaeans, the first great Greek-speaking civilization, the historical reality that lay behind the legends of the heroes.

But this discovery also created a profound mystery. The world Homer described was a world of warriors and kings who, for all their squabbles, were part of a single, interconnected culture. Yet, sometime around 1200 B.C., this entire civilization vanished. Its mighty palaces were burned to the ground. Its intricate bureaucracy disappeared. Its trade networks were severed. And most remarkably, its people forgot how to write. The complex Linear B script, used by the palace scribes to manage their kingdoms, disappeared so completely that it would not be deciphered for over three thousand years. The Age of Heroes ended not with a bang, but with a sudden, deafening silence. A "Dark Age" descended upon Greece, a four-hundred-year period of poverty, isolation, and illiteracy.

The fall of the Mycenaean world was one of the most complete and devastating societal collapses in European history. It was a systems collapse on every level: political, economic, social, and cultural. To understand it, we must walk through the ghostly ruins of the heroes' citadels, decipher the final, frantic records of their scribes, and confront the terrifying speed with which a complex civilization can unravel, leaving behind only the faintest echo of its former glory in the verses of a blind poet.

THE END OF THE HEROES

A World of Warrior-Bureaucrats

To understand what was lost, we must first picture the Mycenaean world at its peak in the 14th and 13th centuries B.C. It was not a single, unified empire like Egypt. It was a collection of independent palace-states, a network of rival kingdoms centered on formidable, fortified citadels like Mycenae, Pylos, Tiryns, Thebes, and Athens. The rulers of these citadels, known in their own language as the *wanax*, were the historical figures who would evolve into the legendary kings of Greek myth.

These were warrior-kings, their culture steeped in a martial ethos. Their art is dominated by scenes of combat: warriors in boar's-tusk helmets, hunters stalking lions, and processions of figure-eight shields. Their graves are filled with weapons: long bronze rapiers, heavy spearheads, and beautifully crafted daggers. They were the masters of the chariot, an elite warrior class whose wealth and power were built on their ability to dominate the battlefield.

But beneath this heroic, warrior exterior lay the same bureaucratic engine we have seen elsewhere. The Mycenaean *wanax* was not just a warlord; he was the CEO of a palace economy. From his great central hall, or *megaron*—a large rectangular room with a massive central hearth and a throne—he presided over a kingdom organized with the obsessive, list-making precision of a modern corporation. As we saw at Pylos, the Linear B scribes were the indispensable managers of this system, meticulously tracking every sheep, every jar of oil, every bronze sword, and every textile worker in the kingdom.

This system generated enormous wealth. The Mycenaeans were major players in the international trade of the Glimmering World. Their distinctive, finely-made pottery is found all over the Eastern Mediterranean, from Sicily to Syria. They imported copper, tin, gold, ivory, and glass, which their skilled artisans transformed into the luxury goods that adorned the palaces and filled the tombs of the elite. They were a vital part of the globalized Bronze Age economy, a wealthy and powerful civilization at the northwestern edge of the Great Club's world.

Their engineering prowess was astounding. The citadel of Mycenae, perched on a rocky hill commanding the plain of Argos, is a masterpiece of military architecture. It is encircled by the famous Cyclopean walls, a fortification over half a mile long, up to twenty-five feet thick, and built with unworked limestone boulders weighing several tons each. The main entrance, the magnificent Lion Gate, is topped by a single lintel block estimated to weigh twenty tons. This was a society capable of organizing and commanding immense labor resources, a society that believed in its own power and permanence.

And yet, it was all a house of cards. The Mycenaean palace system, like its counterparts in the Near East, was a top-heavy, centralized, and deeply brittle machine. Its wealth was concentrated in the hands of a tiny elite. Its economy was utterly dependent on agricultural surplus and the uninterrupted flow of international trade. It was a system perfectly adapted for the stable climate and political conditions of the 14th century, but dangerously ill-equipped to handle the systemic shocks that were coming.

The Walls Go Up

The first sign that something was deeply wrong in the Mycenaean world is written in stone. Around the middle of the 13th century B.C., a wave of anxiety seems to have swept through Greece. The great palace centers began to engage in a massive, almost frantic, program of defensive construction. This was not the normal, piecemeal strengthening of fortifications; this was a coordinated, system-wide effort to turn the citadels into impregnable fortresses.

At Mycenae, the Cyclopean walls were extended to enclose the southern slope of the acropolis, protecting the grave circle where the city's founding kings were buried. More importantly, a secret, subterranean passage was constructed, a remarkable feat of engineering called the "Sally Port." It was a corbel-vaulted tunnel that led sixty feet down, through ninety-nine stone steps, to a hidden underground cistern dug deep into the rock outside the main walls. This guaranteed the citadel a secure water supply in the event of a long siege.

At nearby Tiryns, the fortifications were even more impressive. The walls were expanded to a thickness of over thirty feet in places, creating a series of heavily defended gates and narrow, enclosed passages designed to trap attackers in a deadly crossfire. Like Mycenae, Tiryns also built an elaborate underground passage leading to a protected water source. On the Acropolis of Athens, which was a major Mycenaean center at the time, a similar project was undertaken to secure the water supply.

This sudden, widespread obsession with fortification and water security is a clear symptom of a society under immense stress. Who were they so afraid of? The traditional explanation was that they were preparing for rival Mycenaean states. But the sheer scale and synchronicity of the construction suggest a more universal threat. These were not walls built against a known enemy like the king of a neighboring city. These were walls built against a new and terrifying kind of insecurity.

The threat was likely twofold. As we have seen, the climate was changing. The onset of drought would have put immense pressure on food and water resources, leading to internal unrest. The walls may have been as much about protecting the palace elite from their own hungry populace as from any external foe. The secret cisterns were a guarantee that the *wanax* and his court would have water, even if the farmers in the lower town were dying of thirst.

But the fortifications also point to a new external military threat. These were defenses designed to withstand a siege by a powerful and determined enemy. Perhaps the Mycenaeans were receiving panicked reports from their trading partners in the East. Perhaps they had seen the first pirate fleets of the Lukka or Sherden probing the Aegean islands. The Heroic Age was becoming an Age of Fear, and the kings were retreating into their stone shells, desperately trying to wall out a world that was becoming increasingly hostile and unpredictable.

The Fires of Pylos

The walls, in the end, did not save them. Sometime between 1200 and 1180 B.C., the storm broke over Greece. One by one, the great palace centers were destroyed in a wave of violent conflagrations. The evidence is universal and unambiguous: every major Mycenaean citadel, from Pylos in the west to Mycenae and Tiryns in the east, went up in flames.

The destruction of the Palace of Nestor at Pylos is perhaps the best-documented and most poignant case. As we saw earlier, the final administrative records of the palace, the Linear B tablets, show a kingdom in a state of high alert. The scribes were meticulously recording the dispatch of coastal watchers, the mobilization of naval rowers, and the collection of bronze for weapon manufacturing. They were a bureaucracy preparing for war.

The archaeology of the site tells the story of their failure. The destruction was sudden and total. The palace was consumed by a fire so intense that it vitrified pottery, turned clay tablets into brick, and left a thick layer of ash and carbonized debris across the entire hilltop. The fire was not accidental. It was a deliberate act of destruction.

Imagine the final day. The coastal watchers have sent the dreaded signal: a fleet of enemy ships has been sighted. But this is not a rival Mycenaean king's army, whose tactics would be understood. These are strangers, perhaps the same sea-raiders who have been terrorizing the coasts for years, but now in overwhelming numbers. The Pylian fleet, hastily assembled, is no match for them. The invaders beach their ships and surge inland.

The palace at Pylos, unlike Mycenae or Tiryns, was not heavily fortified. Its power lay in its economic control and its naval strength, not in massive walls. The defense is valiant but hopeless. The invaders storm the hill, overwhelming the palace guards. The fighting spills into the courtyards and the great megaron. The invaders are not interested in capturing the palace intact; their goal is annihilation. They put the torch to the brightly painted walls and the cedar-wood columns.

Inside the archives, the scribes are still at their posts, perhaps trying to save the precious records, when the smoke and flames engulf them. The fire, fed by the thousands of gallons of olive oil stored in the palace magazines, becomes an inferno. The roof collapses, burying the archives and their keepers. The Palace of Nestor, the center of a thriving kingdom for over a century, is reduced to a smoking, blackened ruin in a matter of hours.

Who were the destroyers? The question has haunted archaeologists for generations. There are no bodies of foreign invaders, no distinctive weapons of a new people. This has led some scholars to argue for an internal cause. Perhaps the destroyers were not foreigners at all, but the kingdom's own oppressed populace—the farmers and laborers, driven to revolt by years of drought and the relentless demands of the palace. In this scenario, the destruction of Pylos was a peasant uprising, a bloody, revolutionary act to overthrow the ruling elite.

This theory is compelling, as it accounts for the lack of foreign artifacts. But it doesn't fully explain the synchronous destruction of all the other palace centers. It seems more likely that the truth is a combination of both factors. The internal unrest created by the drought and the palace system's failures had fatally weakened the Mycenaean kingdoms. They were hollowed out from within. This made them fatally vulnerable to the external shock delivered by the sea-borne raiders who were themselves a product of the same regional crisis. It was a perfect storm of internal revolt and external attack.

A Cascade of Collapse

The fall of Pylos was not an isolated event. It was the beginning of a domino effect. The destruction of one palace center sent shockwaves through the entire network. The highly specialized, interdependent Mycenaean world began to unravel.

The great citadel of Mycenae, despite its colossal walls, also fell. The destruction here seems to have happened in stages, with an earlier earthquake causing significant damage before a final, fiery destruction around 1190 B.C. The houses of wealthy merchants and officials outside the main citadel walls were burned and looted. Tiryns, Gla, Iolcos—the story is the same everywhere. A wave of violence swept across the Greek mainland, extinguishing the lights of civilization one by one.

The collapse was total. It was not just the palaces that were destroyed, but the entire system they represented. The complex palace economy, with its tribute-based redistribution, vanished. The international trade routes were severed. The flow of copper, tin, and luxury goods from the East ceased. Without the palace to organize production, the specialized crafts that had defined Mycenaean culture—fresco painting, ivory carving, fine metalwork—disappeared.

The social structure was decapitated. The *wanax* and his court, the elite *maryannu* warriors, the scribal class—all were either killed in the destruction or scattered, their power and privilege evaporating overnight. Without the elite to patronize them, the artists and craftsmen had no work. Without the palace to organize them, the farmers reverted to subsistence agriculture.

And most profoundly, the knowledge of writing was lost. The Linear B script was a specialist tool, used exclusively by the palace bureaucracy for its own administrative purposes. It was never a script used for literature, private letters, or public inscriptions. When the palaces and the scribal class that inhabited them were destroyed, the script had no reason to exist. It vanished from the face of the earth, a casualty of the system's own hyper-specialization.

Imagine a modern society where, after a great catastrophe, the only people who knew how to read and write were corporate accountants, and all they had ever written were internal company spreadsheets. If that entire corporate structure collapsed, the art of writing itself might vanish. This is what happened in Greece. The loss was so complete that when the Greeks re-emerged into literacy four centuries later, they did not rediscover Linear B. They adopted a completely new and far simpler system, the alphabet, from their new trading partners, the Phoenicians.

The Long Dark Age

What followed the collapse was a period that historians, for want of a better term, call the Greek Dark Age. It was not "dark" because the people were primitive or unintelligent, but because the archaeological record becomes suddenly impoverished, and the light of written history is extinguished.

The population of Greece plummeted. Estimates suggest that the population may have declined by as much as 75 percent. The great citadels were abandoned, or inhabited only by a few squatters living in the ruins of former glory. The population dispersed into small, isolated, and impoverished villages. Life became smaller, more local, more rural.

The material culture reflects this impoverishment. The finely decorated pottery of the Mycenaean era was replaced by crude, simple, and undecorated wares. The grand stone tombs of the kings were replaced by simple pit graves with few, if any, grave goods. The knowledge of building in stone on a large scale was lost. The vibrant, colorful frescoes disappeared. The world became, in a tangible, archaeological sense, grayer.

This was a world without kings, without palaces, without scribes. It was a world of petty chieftains and small-scale subsistence farming. The great international connections were gone. For four hundred years, Greece was essentially cut off from the rest of the world, a cultural backwater struggling to survive.

But it was not a complete void. In the darkness, something survived: memory. The stories of the great age before the collapse—the tales of the mighty kings, the great walls, and the epic war across the sea at Troy—were kept alive. They were passed down not on clay tablets, but through the oral poetry of bards, singers of tales who performed in the humble halls of Dark Age chieftains.

These stories, altered and embellished with each retelling, became the foundation of a new Greek identity. They were a link to a lost, heroic past, a source of pride and inspiration in a diminished present. The memory of Agamemnon and Achilles, of Pylos and Mycenae, became the seed from which a new civilization would eventually grow.

When Homer composed the *Iliad* and the *Odyssey* at the very end of this Dark Age, around 750 B.C., he was not just creating a work of literature. He was gathering up the fragmented memories of the lost Mycenaean world and weaving them into a coherent epic. He was giving a voice to the silent ruins, transforming the dimly remembered *wanax* into a legendary hero, and the brutal, chaotic collapse into a timeless story of glory, tragedy, and human endurance.

The end of the heroes was, in this sense, also their beginning. The fiery destruction of their palaces was a necessary precondition for their rebirth as figures of myth. The collapse wiped the slate clean, creating the cultural space for a new kind of society to emerge, one that would be built not on the rigid, top-down model of the palace economy, but on the more decentralized and dynamic concept of the *polis*, or city-state.

The fall of the Mycenaean world stands as a stark and terrifying reminder of the fragility of civilization. It shows how quickly a complex, wealthy, and seemingly powerful society can unravel. The loss was profound—a loss of population, of technology, of art, of literacy. It was a descent into a long and difficult darkness. But it was also, in the long run, a creative destruction. From the ashes of the heroes' palaces, a new Greek world would eventually be born, a world that would remember its heroic past, but would choose to build a very different future. The silence would end, and the voices that emerged from it would, in time, come to shape the foundations of Western civilization itself.

10

The Phantom Empire

In the grand narrative of the Bronze Age, there were two pillars that held up the world. Two superpowers, two titans, whose rivalry and correspondence had defined the international order for centuries. One was Egypt, the eternal kingdom, nourished by the predictable bounty of the Nile. The other was the Hittite Empire, a formidable and complex power that had risen from the harsh, high plateau of Anatolia to conquer a vast domain stretching from the Aegean Sea to the gates of Babylon. They were the yin and yang of the Glimmering World, the great rivals of Kadesh, the "Brothers" of the peace treaty.

When the great storm of the collapse finally broke, Egypt, though battered and diminished, survived. It repelled the invaders, recorded its victories, and lived on to tell the tale.

The Hittite Empire simply vanished.

This is perhaps the most baffling and profound mystery of the entire Bronze Age Collapse. We are not talking about the slow decline of a fading power. We are talking about the sudden, wholesale disappearance of a superpower from the stage of history. One moment, the Hittite king is a major player, commanding vast armies, receiving tribute from dozens of vassal states, and corresponding as an equal with the Pharaoh. The next moment, there is only silence. The capital city is a smoking ruin. The royal line is extinguished. The very name of Hatti fades from the memory of the world for over three thousand years. It is as if a modern superpower, with its sprawling cities, its military bases, and its global influence, were to evaporate in the space of a single generation, leaving behind only burned-out buildings and a handful of garbled refugee accounts.

The end of the Hittite Empire was not a defeat; it was a deletion. It was the most complete and spectacular systems collapse of the era. The quest to understand how this phantom empire disappeared takes us to its rugged heartland, to the windswept ruins of its mighty capital, where we must sift through the rubble and weigh the evidence in a cold case that is three millennia old. Was it a victim of foreign invasion, internal rebellion, or a biblical famine? Or was the truth something even stranger, a deliberate and desperate vanishing act in the face of an unstoppable catastrophe?

The Land of a Thousand Gods

To comprehend the fall, we must first appreciate the titan that fell. The Hittite Empire was a unique and formidable creation, a testament to the resilience of a people who carved a world-class power out of a challenging and unforgiving landscape. Unlike Egypt, with its single, life-giving river, the

Hittite heartland in central Anatolia was a high, dry plateau, with harsh winters and rain-fed agriculture that was always at the mercy of the climate. This environment bred a people who were tough, pragmatic, and adaptable.

Their capital city, Hattusa, was a statement of their character. Perched on a rocky spur overlooking a gorge, it was a fortress city on a scale that dwarfed its Mycenaean counterparts. At its peak, the city was enclosed by a massive double wall of stone and mudbrick that ran for over four miles, punctuated by heavily defended gates that were themselves works of monumental art. The King's Gate, the Lion Gate, and the Sphinx Gate, with their powerful, apotropaic sculptures designed to ward off evil, were the intimidating public face of a military and administrative powerhouse.

Within these walls was a complex city of temples, palaces, archives, and residential quarters. The Hittites called their land "the land of a thousand gods," and their capital reflected this. It was a great religious center, home to dozens of temples dedicated to the vast and diverse pantheon they had assembled from the various peoples they had conquered. The king was not a living god like the Pharaoh, but the high priest and chief steward of the Storm God of Hatti, the supreme deity who brought the life-giving rains. This was a crucial role, and a king's legitimacy was tied directly to his ability to ensure the gods were pleased and the land was fertile—a connection that would become a fatal liability.

The Hittites were innovators. While they did not invent iron smelting, they were among the earliest and most skilled ironworkers of their time, and their rare iron objects were considered gifts worthy of a pharaoh. They were masters of law and diplomacy, as the intricate clauses of the Treaty of

Kadesh attest. And they were relentless warriors. Their chariot corps, as we have seen, was the terror of the ancient world. This was a sophisticated, literate, and deeply pious civilization that had every reason to believe in its own permanence. They had conquered the kingdom of Mitanni, sacked the legendary city of Babylon, and fought the mighty Egyptian empire to a standstill. They were, by any measure, one of the two most powerful nations on earth. And then they were gone.

A Tour of the Crime Scene

Our investigation begins at the ruins of Hattusa. Today, it is a UNESCO World Heritage site, a haunting landscape of stone foundations, scattered column bases, and lonely gates staring out over the Anatolian plain. But for the archaeologist, it is a crime scene, and every stone tells a story of the city's final, violent moments.

Excavations across the vast site reveal a universal and unambiguous picture: sometime around 1180 B.C., the city was utterly destroyed by fire. A thick, uniform burn layer covers the entire city, from the grandest temples on the acropolis to the humblest houses in the lower town. The heat of the conflagration was so intense that it turned the city's mud-brick superstructures into red, vitrified slag. The great stone statues of the gods in the temples were toppled and sometimes deliberately smashed. The monumental gates were burned and choked with rubble. The destruction was not partial or accidental; it was total and deliberate. This was an act of annihilation.

So, the cause of death seems simple: a catastrophic fire, likely set by a conquering enemy. Case closed. But this is where the mystery deepens. A closer look at the crime scene reveals a series of baffling and contradictory clues.

First, despite the evidence of a violent end, there is a distinct lack of bodies. In a city of an estimated 40,000 to 50,000 people, one would expect to find evidence of a great battle or a mass slaughter—mass graves, skeletons lying in the streets, soldiers cut down at their posts. But very few human remains have been found in the destruction layer at Hattusa. This suggests that the city was largely, if not entirely, empty when the final destruction occurred.

Second, there is a scarcity of valuable, portable objects. While the invaders toppled statues, they do not seem to have engaged in systematic looting. The palaces and temples were not filled with the treasures one would expect from a royal capital. It is as if the city had already been stripped of its wealth before the arsonists arrived.

Third, and most tellingly, there is the mystery of the archives. Hattusa has yielded thousands of clay tablets, the state records that have allowed us to reconstruct Hittite history. But these archives seem to have been tidied up. There are no last, frantic letters like those found in the kiln at Ugarit. The great literary works, the historical annals, the royal decrees—many of these seem to have been carefully stored or, more likely, removed. The state did not die in mid-sentence. It appears to have packed its bags.

These clues point to a mind-boggling scenario: the end of Hattusa was not the storming of a thriving capital, but the torching of a ghost town. It seems the last Hittite king and his court deliberately abandoned their capital city, taking the state treasury, the sacred idols of the gods, the archival records, and a significant portion of the population with them, before an enemy arrived to deliver the final, pointless blow.

Why would they do this? And who was the enemy they were fleeing? To answer this, we must weigh the prime suspects in the murder of the Hittite Empire.

Suspect #1: The Kaska

For the entire history of the Hittite Empire, their greatest and most persistent security threat came from the north. The Pontic Mountains that bordered the Black Sea were home to a group of fierce, non-literate, tribal peoples known collectively as the Kaska. The Kaska were to the Hittites what the barbarians were to the Romans: a constant, disruptive presence on their northern frontier. They were raiders, not conquerors. They would sweep down from their mountain strongholds to pillage Hittite towns and farms, and then retreat back into the hills where the Hittite chariot armies could not follow.

Hittite annals are a monotonous litany of campaigns against the Kaska. Nearly every Hittite king, from the earliest to the last, had to march north to try and pacify these unruly tribes. They could be defeated in battle, but they could never be truly conquered or assimilated. They were a permanent, bleeding ulcer on the northern flank of the empire.

It is entirely plausible, even likely, that a Kaska army delivered the final blow to Hattusa. As the Hittite state weakened from drought and internal strife, its control over the northern frontier would have dissolved. The Kaska, seeing their ancient enemy on its knees, would have seized the opportunity. They could have swept down from the mountains, found the capital city largely deserted, and indulged in an orgy of destruction, burning the hated symbols of an empire that had oppressed them for centuries.

The Kaska are an excellent candidate for the role of the arsonist. But they cannot explain the mystery of the empty city. They were raiders, not a replacement civilization. Their goal was plunder and destruction, not the overthrow and occupation of the state. They were the vultures who descended on the carcass, but they were not the cause of death.

Suspect #2: The Sea Peoples

Could the mysterious Sea Peoples have been responsible? The final Hittite king, Šuppiluliuma II, recorded a naval victory against the ships of Alashiya (Cyprus), which were likely allied with Sea Peoples groups. We know from the Ugaritic letters that seafaring enemies—the Shikila—were active along the coast. It is tempting to imagine a great wave of these invaders sweeping up from the Mediterranean coast and penetrating deep into the Anatolian plateau to destroy Hattusa.

However, the geography makes this difficult. Hattusa is over 150 miles from the sea, separated by rugged mountain ranges. This is a long and difficult march for a naval-based force. More importantly, the archaeological evidence at Hattusa shows no trace of the distinctive material culture—the pottery, the weapons, the feathered headdresses—associated with the Sea

Peoples in the Egyptian reliefs or in the Philistine settlements of Canaan. If the Sea Peoples sacked Hattusa, they left no fingerprints at the crime scene.

It is more likely that the Sea Peoples played an indirect, but crucial, role. Their relentless attacks on the coastal regions of the Hittite Empire—the wealthy port cities of the Levant and southern Anatolia—would have severed the empire's vital trade routes. This would have cut off the flow of imported goods, particularly the grain that the starving Hittite heartland so desperately needed. The Sea Peoples effectively imposed a naval blockade, strangling the empire from the sea, even if they never marched on its capital. They helped to create the conditions of famine and isolation that made the final collapse inevitable.

Suspect #3: Famine, Plague, and Internal Collapse

The most compelling suspect in the death of the Hittite Empire is the empire itself. The evidence strongly suggests that the Hittite state did not fall to an external enemy, but imploded under the weight of its own internal crises, with environmental catastrophe as the primary catalyst.

As we have established, the Hittite heartland was uniquely vulnerable to the megadrought that struck the region. The desperate letters begging for grain are the smoking gun. A state that cannot feed its people is a state that has lost its reason to exist. The king's legitimacy was tied to the Storm God and the promise of fertility. A multi-generational drought was a sign that the gods had abandoned the king and the land.

Famine on this scale would have triggered a cascade of secondary crises. The army, unpaid and unfed, would have dissolved. The population, faced with starvation, would have risen in revolt or simply fled, becoming refugees and joining outlaw bands. The carefully constructed multi-ethnic empire, held together by treaties and military force, would have disintegrated as vassal states declared their independence and old rivalries flared.

Disease would have followed famine. Malnourished populations are breeding grounds for epidemics. It is highly likely that plagues swept through the starving cities, further decimating the population and accelerating the collapse.

This brings us to the most plausible scenario for the final days of Hattusa. The last king, Šuppiluliuma II, was not a passive victim. He was the captain of a sinking ship, facing an impossible situation. His land was barren, his people were starving, his vassals were in revolt, the Kaska were pressing from the north, and the Sea Peoples were strangling his coastline. He realized that the heartland was no longer defensible or sustainable. Hattusa, the great capital, had become a death trap.

So, he made a radical and desperate decision: he organized a strategic retreat. He would abandon the ancestral capital and attempt to move the core of the Hittite state—the royal court, the state treasury, the transportable religious idols, the essential administrative archives, and the loyal segments of the population—to a new, more secure location. The most likely destination was northern Syria, in the region of Carchemish, a major Hittite stronghold on the Euphrates River, which was more agriculturally stable and defensible.

This was not the flight of a defeated king. It was a calculated, albeit desperate, attempt to preserve the Hittite state by amputating its dying heartland. This theory elegantly explains the strange evidence at the crime scene: the empty city, the lack of bodies, the missing treasures and archives. The Hittites abandoned their capital before their enemies could take it. The final, fiery destruction was an afterthought, the torching of an empty shell by opportunistic Kaska or other local enemies after the soul of the city had already departed.

The Afterlife of a Phantom

Did the plan work? Yes and no. The great, centralized Hittite Empire was gone forever. The imperial structure, the brotherhood of Great Kings, the very concept of Hatti as a world power—all of it vanished. In this sense, the collapse was total.

But the Hittite people and their culture did not entirely disappear. The managed retreat, if that is what it was, succeeded in preserving a spark of the Hittite legacy. In the centuries that followed the fall of Hattusa, a constellation of smaller kingdoms arose in southern Anatolia and northern Syria. We call these the "Neo-Hittite" or "Syro-Hittite" states.

These kingdoms, centered on cities like Carchemish, Malatya, and Zincirli, carried on the traditions of the lost empire. Their rulers bore Hittite names. They worshipped Hittite gods. And crucially, they continued to use a form of the Hittite language, written not in the old cuneiform script of the palace scribes, but in a unique and beautiful monumental script known as Luwian hieroglyphs. This script, once used for royal inscriptions, became the primary written language of these successor states.

The Neo-Hittite kingdoms were a shadow of the former empire. They were small, regional powers, often paying tribute to the new superpowers of the Iron Age, the Assyrians and Babylonians. But they were a living link to the Bronze Age past. They were the afterlife of the phantom empire. For several hundred years, they kept the flame of Hittite culture alive, until they were eventually absorbed into the great empires of the first millennium B.C. and the name of the Hittites was finally, truly forgotten, until their rediscovery by modern archaeology.

The baffling disappearance of the Hittite Empire is thus not a simple story of conquest. It is a complex and tragic tale of a perfect storm. It was a civilization killed by a thousand cuts: by a relentless drought that starved its people and delegitimized its king; by the slow bleed of perennial warfare on its frontiers; by the stranglehold of pirates and raiders on its economic lifelines; and by the internal decay of a system that could no longer hold. The final destruction of its capital was not the cause of the collapse; it was its tombstone.

The phantom empire serves as the ultimate cautionary tale of the Bronze Age. It demonstrates, more clearly than any other case, how even the most powerful, sophisticated, and seemingly invincible states can be brought down by a convergence of environmental, social, and political crises. It shows that no wall is high enough, no army strong enough, to defeat an enemy as fundamental as a change in the climate. The Hittites, the great rivals of Egypt, the conquerors of Babylon, were ultimately conquered by the sky and the earth. Their empire did not just fall; it dissolved, leaving a ghost-shaped hole in the map of the world.

11

The Face of the Enemy

For a century, they have been the ghosts in our story, the spectral architects of ruin. We have heard their names whispered in the panicked dispatches of kings and the frantic letters of scribes. We have seen the trail of their destruction in the uniform ash layers of burned cities, from the windy plains of Troy to the sun-drenched coast of Syria. They are the great enigma of the Bronze Age, the shadowy villains universally accused of bringing an entire, glittering world to its knees. They are the Foreign Peoples of the Sea.

Now, at last, the time for whispers is over. We come face to face with them. After sifting through the evidence of a world in its death throes—a world wracked by climate change, shattered by earthquakes, and hollowed out by internal decay—we must finally confront the agents who delivered the final, fatal blow. Our primary guide on this journey, our star witness, is the man who claimed to have met them, defeated them, and single-handedly saved civilization from their onslaught: the Pharaoh Ramesses III.

On the massive, sun-baked stone walls of his mortuary

temple at Medinet Habu, Ramesses has left us the most detailed, dramatic, and deeply problematic portrait of these mysterious invaders that exists. It is here, in the glorious, propagandistic war reliefs commissioned by the victorious pharaoh, that we can finally look our mystery villains in the eye. This is the great reveal.

But this chapter is not merely an exercise in identification, a simple line-up of ancient suspects. It is an interrogation. We must question our star witness, for he is far from impartial. We must deconstruct his testimony, separating the hard facts from the heroic fiction. Who were these people with their strange, feathered headdresses and their menacing, horned helmets? Were they a unified, conquering army, a barbarian horde bent on pure destruction, as Ramesses's inscriptions would have us believe? Or were they something far more complex, something far more tragic?

As we peel back the layers of pharaonic propaganda and combine the images on the temple walls with the scattered clues from archaeology, linguistics, and other ancient texts, a new and astonishing picture emerges. The simple, monstrous villain begins to dissolve, replaced by a gallery of human faces, etched with desperation. What we find is not a single, malevolent force, but a reflection of the broken world we have already explored. The Sea Peoples were not an army. They were a phenomenon. They were a chaotic, heterogeneous coalition of displaced peoples, opportunistic pirates, land-hungry migrants, and renegade mercenaries. They were both the final cause of the collapse and its most visible, tragic symptom. They were, in the end, the human face of the perfect storm.

The Temple as an Eternal Machine

To understand the testimony, we must first understand the witness and his motivations. Medinet Habu is not a history book. It is a machine for eternity. To an ancient Egyptian, a mortuary temple was not a passive memorial; it was a divine engine, a sacred stage where the rituals performed by priests would perpetually fuel the pharaoh's soul in the afterlife. But it was also an engine of propaganda, designed to broadcast a specific, state-sanctioned version of reality not just to his subjects and successors, but to the gods themselves.

When you stand before the northern outer wall today, the sheer scale is overwhelming. The sandstone reliefs stretch for over 180 feet, a vast, cinematic narrative carved in stone. The early European explorers who first documented the site in the 19th century, men like Jean-François Champollion, who had just cracked the code of the hieroglyphs, were stunned. Here was a story of a great war, as epic as anything in Homer, but told from the Egyptian point of view. It was a story of cosmic significance.

In Egyptian ideology, the world existed in a state of *ma'at*—a concept embodying order, truth, and justice. The pharaoh's primary role was to uphold *ma'at* and defend it against the forces of *isfet*, or chaos, which constantly threatened from beyond Egypt's borders. Foreigners, particularly those who challenged the pharaoh's rule, were the physical embodiment of *isfet*. The reliefs at Medinet Habu are therefore not just a record of a battle; they are a theological statement. They depict the divine pharaoh, the champion of *ma'at*, vanquishing the chaotic hordes from the sea and restoring the balance of the cosmos. This is the story Ramesses III *needed* to tell, to secure his legacy both on earth and in the heavens. Our task is to find the history that lies buried beneath the theology.

A Rogues' Gallery Carved in Stone

Let us now step closer to the wall and examine the enemy. The Egyptian artists, with their characteristic eye for detail, have given us a veritable catalogue of chaos, a rogues' gallery of the peoples who made up this invading force. In the grandiloquent inscriptions that accompany the reliefs, Ramesses III gives us a specific list: "Their confederation was the Peleset, Tjekker, Shekelesh, Denyen, and Weshesh, lands united." By cross-referencing this list with the distinct visual depictions in the reliefs, we can begin to assemble a profile for each of these mysterious groups.

The Peleset

The most prominent and frequently depicted of all the Sea Peoples are the Peleset. They are the stars of the show. Their most striking feature is a distinctive headdress, a high, circular crown that appears to be made of upright, parallel bands. For years, scholars have debated its construction. Is it a ring of feathers, as it is often described? Or perhaps stiffened leather strips, reeds woven together, or even horsehair treated to stand upright? Whatever its material, it is a unique and instantly recognizable marker. It gives them a proud, almost regal bearing, even in defeat.

They are shown as tall, clean-shaven men with sharp features. They wear short, belted kilts, often with intricate, woven patterns. Over their chests, they wear a sophisticated corselet, seemingly made of overlapping bronze plates or hardened leather strips, designed to protect the torso. Their primary weapons are long, straight swords, a significant departure from the Egyptian sickle-sword, and heavy thrusting spears. For defense, they carry round shields of a type more common in the Aegean than the Near East.

The Peleset are the group most clearly associated with the migrating families. It is their warriors who form the main line of battle in the land relief, and it is their women and children who are shown huddled in the cumbersome oxcarts just behind the fighting. This is our first great clue: the Peleset were not just a band of warriors; they were a nation on the move.

And their story does not end at Medinet Habu. The Peleset are, by near-universal scholarly consensus, the people who would become known to history as the Philistines. After their defeat, a contingent of them were settled by the Egyptians on the southern coast of Canaan, in a string of five cities that would become the famous Philistine Pentapolis: Gaza, Ashkelon, Ashdod, Gath, and Ekron.

It is here that archaeology picks up their trail. In the destruction layers of the old Canaanite cities, a new and vibrant material culture appears. Most distinctive is a beautiful type of pottery known as Philistine Bichrome ware, decorated with geometric patterns and, most tellingly, stylized birds, often in panels, a decorative style that has its closest parallels in the

Mycenaean pottery of the late Aegean Bronze Age.

The Peleset, it seems, brought their potters and their artistic traditions with them. Their arrival in Canaan, as a settled and powerful people, would forever alter the political landscape of the Levant and set the stage for their famous, centuries-long conflict with the emerging kingdom of Israel, as chronicled in the Hebrew Bible. The giant Goliath, in his bronze helmet and coat of mail, may well have been a distant descendant of the warriors depicted on the walls of Medinet Habu.

The Tjekker

Visually, the Tjekker are the close cousins of the Peleset. They are often depicted wearing the same "feathered" headdress and carrying similar arms. This has led some to suggest they were a closely related tribe, or perhaps a subordinate group within a Peleset-led coalition. Their name, however, is distinct, and they appear in later texts as an independent people.

Our most vivid portrait of the Tjekker comes from a remarkable Egyptian document known as the *Story of Wenamun*, written about a century after the reign of Ramesses III. It is the travelogue of an Egyptian priest, Wenamun, who is sent on a mission to the city of Byblos to acquire cedar wood for a sacred barge. The story is a catalogue of humiliations, a perfect illustration of Egypt's diminished status in the post-collapse world. At one point, Wenamun's ship docks at the port of Dor, on the coast just south of modern-day Haifa. Dor, he tells us, is a "town of the Tjekker."

Here, he has a tense encounter with the local Tjekker prince, a man named Beder. Wenamun is robbed by one of his own crewmen, and he demands that Beder find the thief and restore his stolen gold and silver. Beder's response is a masterclass in bureaucratic indifference. He tells Wenamun that if the thief were one of his own people, he would of course pay him back. But since the thief is one of Wenamun's own crew, it's not his problem. The once-mighty Egyptian envoy is left powerless and fuming. The story reveals that the Tjekker, like the Peleset, had successfully settled on the Levantine coast, establishing their own independent city-states and controlling the maritime trade. The former sea-raiders had become rulers in their own right.

The Shekelesh and the Sherden: The Western Connection?

The next two groups in our gallery, the Shekelesh and the Sherden, draw our gaze far to the west, to the islands of the Central Mediterranean. The Shekelesh are less clearly defined in the reliefs, but their name has long been associated with Sicily. The Sherden, on the other hand, are unmistakable. They are the warriors with the iconic horned helmets. As we have seen, they had a long history as both pirates and elite mercenaries in the Egyptian army. Their name is so close to Sardinia that the connection seems almost undeniable.

Is this just a linguistic coincidence? Archaeology provides tantalizing, if not conclusive, support. In Sardinia, the indigenous Nuragic civilization of the Bronze Age produced thousands of remarkable bronze figurines, known as *bronzetti*.

Among these are numerous depictions of warriors. They carry round shields. They wield long, straight swords. And most strikingly, some of them wear helmets adorned with a pair of prominent horns. The resemblance to the Sherden of the Egyptian reliefs is uncanny. It is entirely possible that Sardinia was either the ancestral homeland of the Sherden or the place they ultimately settled after the chaos of the collapse.

The story of the Sherden encapsulates the chaotic, opportunistic nature of the age. They were the ultimate soldiers of fortune. We see them fighting *against* Ramesses II in his early years, then serving as his elite bodyguard at the Battle of Kadesh. In the time of Merneptah, they are listed among the sea-borne invaders allied with the Libyans. And at the great battle under Ramesses III, it is almost certain they were fighting on both sides—as loyal mercenaries in the Egyptian ranks and as members of the invading Sea Peoples coalition. Their allegiance was not to a nation or a king, but to warfare itself. They were a military brotherhood who would fight for anyone who could pay them, or fight for themselves if no better offer was available.

The Denyen and the Ekwesh: The Greek Connection?

Perhaps the most explosive and controversial identifications concern the Denyen and a related group from the earlier invasion under Merneptah, the Ekwesh. The Denyen are depicted as formidable warriors, sometimes with horned helmets, sometimes with simple skullcaps. Their name is strikingly similar to the *Danuna*, a kingdom known from

Hittite texts to be located in Cilicia (southeastern Anatolia). But another, more compelling theory connects them to the *Danaoi*, one of the three names Homer consistently uses for the Greek forces who fought at Troy (the other two being *Achaeans* and *Argives*).

The case for the Ekwesh being Greeks is even stronger. The victory stele of Merneptah, in describing his defeat of the Libyan coalition, lists the Ekwesh among the dead. The inscription adds a unique and fascinating detail: "of the Ekwesh of the countries of the sea, who had no foreskins." This practice of circumcision was common in Egypt and among many Semitic peoples of the Levant, but it was alien to the peoples of the Aegean. The fact that the Egyptian scribe felt it necessary to mention that the Ekwesh were uncircumcised is a powerful cultural marker, pointing directly towards an Aegean origin. Furthermore, the name "Ekwesh" is a plausible Egyptian rendering of *Achaeans* (*Ahhiyawa* in Hittite texts), the most common name for the Mycenaean Greeks.

If these identifications are correct, the implications are staggering. It would mean that contingents of Mycenaean Greeks, their own civilization collapsing around them, their palaces in ruins, their economies shattered by the drought, took to the sea. They became pirates, mercenaries, and migrants, joining a great coalition of other displaced peoples in a desperate attempt to conquer new lands in Libya and Egypt. The heroes of Homer's epics, or at least their descendants, may have ended their days not in a blaze of glory at Troy, but as part of a desperate, failed invasion of the Nile Delta, their bodies left on a foreign battlefield. This theory powerfully links the collapse in Greece with the great migrations of the Sea Peoples, showing them to be two sides of the same catastrophic coin.

Deconstructing the Pharaoh's Victory

Having met the cast of characters, we must now return to the main event: the great land and sea battles as depicted by Ramesses. As we have established, this is war as propaganda. But the propaganda itself is a historical source, revealing the anxieties and priorities of the Egyptian state.

Let's analyze the land battle more closely. The Egyptian army is a vision of perfect, geometric order. The chariots are arrayed in neat lines, the infantry in disciplined blocks. They advance with the inexorable rhythm of a well-oiled machine. Ramesses, god-like in his chariot, leads the charge. The enemy, by contrast, is a chaotic jumble. The Peleset and their allies are a confused mass, their lines broken, their warriors falling over one another. This is a visual representation of *ma'at* versus *isfet*.

But look closer at the details the artists have included. The oxcarts. We have touched on them before, but their significance cannot be overstated. Let us try to imagine the scene from their perspective. A woman, let's call her Iona, huddles in the back of a lurching, solid-wheeled cart, clutching her two small children. The air is thick with dust and the terrifying din of battle—the clash of bronze, the whir of arrows, the screams of men. The cart is piled high with the pathetic remnants of her former life: a few clay pots, a bag of seed corn, a loom that has been taken apart for travel, a roll of woolen blankets.

Her husband, a man who was once a farmer in a land far to the north, is now marching ahead, his face grim, his knuckles white on the shaft of his spear. They have been on the move for years. She has buried another child on the long, hard road through Anatolia. She has seen cities burn. She has lived on the brink of starvation. The stories of the rich, black land of Egypt, the land that never knew famine, had been a beacon of hope, the promise of a new beginning. Now, that hope is being extinguished in a storm of Egyptian arrows. The pharaoh's propaganda depicts her and her family as part of a chaotic, evil force. But from her perspective, they are simply a family that wants to live. The oxcarts are not a military detail; they are a human tragedy, and their inclusion in the relief, perhaps to emphasize the totality of the enemy host, provides the crucial key to understanding the true nature of the Sea Peoples.

Now, let us turn to the naval battle. The scene is a maelstrom of activity in the mouth of the Nile. The Egyptian ships, powered by rowers, are shown systematically destroying the Sea Peoples' fleet. The Egyptian marines, some of them Sherden mercenaries, use grappling hooks to pull the enemy ships close and capsize them. Archers on the shore and on the Egyptian ships rain down arrows on the packed decks of the enemy.

The Sea Peoples' ships are distinctive, with their high, bird-headed prows. As we've noted, they appear to be pure sailing vessels, lacking oars. This made them slaves to the wind. Ramesses's genius was in luring them into the narrow, sheltered channels of the Delta, where the wind was useless and their lack of maneuverability was a fatal weakness. It was like a pod of ocean-going whales being trapped by agile sharks in a shallow, enclosed bay.

The Egyptian artists depict this as a heroic, face-to-face battle. But the reality was likely a massacre, a brilliantly executed ambush that turned the battle into a one-sided slaughter. The Sea Peoples, formidable on the open sea, were helpless in this environment. The propaganda, in its desire to show every detail of the enemy's ships, once again accidentally reveals the tactical brilliance—and brutal efficiency—of the Egyptian victory.

The Verdict: A Confederacy of the Uprooted

So, who were the Sea Peoples? Having sifted through the evidence, we can now offer a final verdict, debunking the myth of a single, mysterious barbarian horde and replacing it with a more complex and historically accurate picture.

First, they were not one people, but many. The term "Sea Peoples" is an external label, an Egyptian catch-all for a diverse and shifting coalition of different ethnic groups. They were the Peleset, the Tjekker, the Shekelesh, the Denyen, the Sherden, and others, each with their own history and identity.

Second, their origins were diverse but broadly "Western" from the Egyptian and Hittite perspective. They came from across the Aegean and the Central Mediterranean—from Greece, Anatolia, Cyprus, and the Italian islands. They were a pan-Mediterranean phenomenon, a testament to a region-wide crisis.

Third, they were set in motion by the perfect storm of crises that brought the Bronze Age to an end. They were the direct human consequence of the climate change, drought, famine, earthquakes, and internal systems collapses that we have traced in the preceding chapters. They were not evil aggressors emerging from a vacuum; they were refugees and survivors of the collapse of their own worlds.

Fourth, their movement was a complex, multi-stage process. It began with opportunistic piracy (the Lukka) and mercenary activity (the Sherden). As the crisis deepened, this escalated into armed mass migration, as entire communities, like the Peleset with their oxcarts, were uprooted and forced to search for new homes.

Fifth, they were both a symptom and a cause of the final collapse. They were a symptom of the chaos in their homelands. But as they moved, their destructive raids on cities like Ugarit shattered the last remaining vestiges of the old international order, creating more chaos and more refugees, thus feeding their own wave.

Finally, they were not an invincible super-army. They were a formidable and desperate fighting force, but they were ultimately defeated by the last great Bronze Age power left standing. Ramesses III's victory was real. The great confederation was broken.

This leads to the ultimate question: if they were defeated, why are they so often blamed for the end of the Bronze Age? Because they were the final, dramatic act in a long and complex play. The stage was already set for tragedy. The Hittite Empire had already imploded. The Mycenaean palaces were already in ruins. The globalized trade network was already shattered. The Sea Peoples did not fell a mighty, healthy oak tree. They were the great storm that blew over a tree that was already rotten to the core. They were the harbingers of a new, darker age, but they were not its sole creators.

The face of the enemy, when we finally see it clearly, is not the face of a monster. It is the face of a desperate human being, caught in the gears of a collapsing world. The story of the

Sea Peoples is a timeless and chilling reminder that the line between refugee and raider, between victim and aggressor, can be perilously thin. It is a story of what happens when the delicate systems that sustain civilization break down, and people are forced to do whatever it takes to survive. The great mystery is solved, and the villain, unmasked, looks disturbingly like ourselves.

IV

Out of the Ashes

Collapse is not an end, but a semicolon. The Bronze Age is a smoking ruin, but in the ashes, survivors huddle, adapt, and innovate. Defeated raiders become nation-builders, and the chaos of collapse gives birth to a radical new world, and a revolutionary new way to write about it.

12

The Long Shadow

The fighting is over. The last of the great cities has fallen, its smoke a final, dark smudge against a silent sky. The tramp of migrating armies fades into the dust of broken roads. The sea, once a highway of empires, grows quiet, its surface reflecting only the slow passage of clouds. The world holds its breath.

This is the morning after. This is the great, terrifying quiet that follows a world-breaking storm. The Bronze Age is dead. But collapse is not a clean ending. It is a messy, lingering state of being. The Glimmering World did not simply vanish; it left a ghost. It cast a long, dark shadow across the centuries, a shadow in which the survivors would have to learn to live, to forget, and to rebuild.

This is our survey of the wreckage. We must now walk through the ghost-haunted landscape of the 11th and 10th centuries B.C., a period historians have aptly named the "Dark Age." The term is not a judgment on the people who lived then, but a reflection of the profound loss that defined their world. It was dark because the great lights of the palace centers had been extinguished. It was dark because the vibrant colors of international trade had faded to a monochrome gray of local subsistence. And it was dark, most literally, because the lamp of literacy had been snuffed out, plunging an entire society into a silent, unlettered world.

To understand what was born from the ashes, we must first comprehend the depth of the loss. We must measure the length of the shadow. This was a smaller, poorer, more rural, and more violent world. It was a world suffering from a kind of collective amnesia, where the complex systems of the past were not just broken, but forgotten. Yet, even in this profound darkness, there were glimmers of light. For this is also a story of human resilience, of the stubborn refusal to surrender. It is the story of how people adapt when the world they knew has been wiped from the map, how they remember, and how, from the humblest of beginnings, they plant the seeds of a new and very different kind of world.

The Great Simplification: A Tour of the Ruins

The most immediate and visible consequence of the collapse was a radical simplification of society. The complex, hierarchical, and urbanized world of the palaces devolved into a landscape of small, isolated, and impoverished villages. The archaeological record tells this story with brutal clarity.

Let us begin our tour in Greece, where the collapse was most total. Imagine a young man, let's call him Diomedes, living around 1100 B.C. His great-grandfather had been a scribe in the Palace of Nestor at Pylos, a man of letters who lived a privileged life within the citadel walls. Now, Diomedes lives with his family in a small, crude hut made of mud-brick and fieldstones, part of a tiny hamlet huddled on a nearby hilltop for defense.

One day, he walks through the ruins of his ancestor's world. The great palace of Pylos is a haunted, overgrown mound of rubble. The colossal stones of its foundation are still there, but the brightly painted frescoes are gone, the cedar-wood pillars are carbonized stumps, and the vast storerooms are empty, their floors littered with the broken shards of thousands of pottery vessels. He sees it not as a palace, but as a place of ghosts, the work of giants or gods from a forgotten age. His world is so far removed from the one that built this place that he cannot even conceive of the social organization it would have required. The shadow of the past is so large, it is incomprehensible.

Diomedes's life is a reflection of this simplification. His family farms a small plot of land, raising enough barley and herding a few goats to feed themselves. There is no king, no *wanax*, to demand tribute. But there is also no one to provide security or distribute grain in a bad year. The largest political unit is his own village, led by a local chieftain, the *basileus*—a word that once meant "king" but now signifies little more than a petty headman.

The material culture reflects this poverty. In his great-grandfather's time, the palace workshops produced exquisite pottery, finely decorated with stylized octopuses and intricate geometric patterns. The cups and bowls in Diomedes's hut are what archaeologists call Submycenaean ware. They are clumsy, misshapen, and almost completely devoid of decoration. They are functional, but joyless. The skill of the master potter, a specialist supported by the palace economy, has been lost. Everyone is now their own potter, their own weaver, their own builder, and they are not very good at it.

His family's graves are simple stone-lined pits, known as cist graves. His great-grandfather would have been buried in a grand chamber tomb, or perhaps even a magnificent beehive-shaped *tholos* tomb, laid to rest with bronze weapons, gold jewelry, and imported ivory. Diomedes's family buries their dead with little more than a single clay pot and a simple bronze pin. The wealth is gone. The belief in a lavish afterlife that needed to be supplied with worldly goods has faded. Survival in *this* life is all that matters.

This picture is repeated across the fallen world. In Anatolia, the mighty Hittite capital of Hattusa is completely abandoned, a ghost city on a windy plateau. The former Hittite heartland is now a patchwork of small, fortified settlements, the population drastically reduced, the grand imperial vision replaced by a narrow focus on local defense.

In the Levant, the ruins of Ugarit lie silent. The survivors of its destruction do not rebuild the great palace or the merchant villas. They scatter. The once-bustling port, the nexus of international trade, is now a deserted bay. Across Canaan, the great Bronze Age city-states—Megiddo, Lachish, Hazor—are all destroyed. The urban civilization that had flourished for two millennia is wiped out. The population becomes overwhelmingly rural, the landscape dotted with small, unfortified farming villages. The long shadow of the collapse is a shadow of shrinking horizons, of a world that has become smaller, poorer, and more isolated.

The Silent Centuries: A World with Amnesia

Of all the losses of the Dark Age, one stands out as the most profound, the most difficult for us, as members of a hyper-literate society, to comprehend. This was the loss of writing. The collapse did not just destroy buildings; it destroyed a fundamental technology of the mind.

In Greece, the disappearance of the Linear B script was sudden and total. As we have seen, this was a direct consequence of its hyper-specialization. Linear B was the exclusive tool of the palace bureaucracy. It was a difficult, cumbersome script with hundreds of signs, requiring years of training. It was used for one thing and one thing only: accounting. It was the software for the palace economy's operating system. When the palaces burned, the scribal schools burned with them. The tiny elite of literate administrators was killed or dispersed. And with the palace system gone, the script had no purpose. It was like a complex piece of code for a computer that no longer existed. It simply vanished.

The consequences of this loss were monumental. It was a form of collective, state-induced amnesia. Without writing, there could be no archives, no state records, no legal codes, no written contracts, no long-distance administrative control. The very possibility of a large, centrally-managed kingdom like those of the Mycenaean era was erased. Society was forced into a simpler, face-to-face mode of existence. Your world was limited to the people you could talk to, your contracts were limited to what could be sealed with a handshake and witnessed by your neighbors, and your history was limited to what the old men of the village could remember.

This plunged Greece into a four-hundred-year silence. We have no texts, no histories, no names of kings or records of events from this entire period. The darkness of the Dark Age is the darkness of a world without its own voice.

How did people cope? They adapted. Culture shifted from the written word to the spoken word. The role of the scribe was replaced by the role of the bard, the singer of tales. Memory became the most prized cultural asset. In the humble, smoky halls of the Dark Age chieftains, these bards would perform the great stories of the age before the darkness. They sang of the great walls of Troy, of the wrath of Achilles, of the ten-year journey of Odysseus. These were not just entertaining stories. They were a lifeline to a lost past, a way of remembering a time when their ancestors were heroes who commanded fleets and lived in golden palaces.

The oral tradition is a fluid thing. The stories were not memorized verbatim. Each bard would recompose the tale in performance, using a stock of memorized formulas and epithets ("swift-footed Achilles," "wine-dark sea"). Over the centuries, the stories changed, were embellished, and were adapted to the values of the Dark Age audience. The bureaucratic, centralized world of the real Mycenaean palaces was forgotten, replaced by a more heroic, individualistic, and feudal society that mirrored the world of the chieftains for whom the bards performed.

This oral tradition is the single most important thread of continuity through the Greek Dark Age. It was the fragile vessel that carried the memory of the Bronze Age across the sea of silence. And at the end of the Dark Age, around 750 B.C., a poet of genius whom we call Homer would gather up these oral traditions and weave them into the two great epic poems that stand at the dawn of Western literature. The *Iliad* and the *Odyssey* are the ultimate product of this long silence, a testament to the power of memory to survive even the most catastrophic collapse.

Elsewhere, the loss of literacy was less absolute, but the decline was still severe. In Anatolia, the complex cuneiform script of the Hittite scribes vanished with the fall of Hattusa. The successor Neo-Hittite states used a different, monumental hieroglyphic script, but its use was far more restricted, mainly for royal inscriptions. The deep, administrative literacy of the Hittite empire was gone. In the Levant, the simple and elegant Ugaritic alphabet also disappeared with the destruction of its home city. It would be left to the Phoenician survivors to reinvent and popularize a similar alphabetic system for a new age. Only in Egypt, where writing was deeply embedded in religion, monumental display, and a continuous scribal tradition, did literacy survive relatively intact, though even there, the quality and volume of literary output declined dramatically. The world had become a much quieter, less literate place.

The Severed Web: The End of Globalization

The ghost of the Uluburun shipwreck haunts the Dark Age. The world that launched that ship—a world of astonishing interconnectedness, where a smith in Greece could use tin from Afghanistan and a queen in Egypt could wear amber from the Baltic—was gone. The defining feature of the collapse was the severing of the web, the catastrophic failure of the first great globalized economy.

The archaeological evidence is stark and undeniable. In the levels of Dark Age sites across Greece and the Levant, imported goods, which were common in the Bronze Age, become vanishingly rare. The flow of copper from Cyprus, the essential ingredient for bronze, slows to a trickle and then stops. The complex supply chain that brought tin from the mountains of Central Asia is completely broken. Without copper and tin, the very production of bronze, the metal that gave the age its name, becomes impossible.

The Bronze Age did not end because a new, superior metal was discovered. It ended because people could no longer make bronze. This was a technological regression forced by the collapse of trade. The magnificent bronze swords, helmets, and corselets of the Mycenaean warrior or the Hittite charioteer could no longer be produced.

This crisis forced a slow, painful, and reluctant transition to a new, and at first, inferior metal: iron. Iron ore, unlike the rare deposits of copper and tin, is one of the most common elements on earth. It was locally available to almost everyone. This was its great advantage. But raw, smelted iron is brittle. To make it useful for tools and weapons, it requires a complex process of carburization (adding carbon) and forging (repeatedly heating and hammering) to create a primitive form of steel. The knowledge of how to do this was not widespread.

The early Iron Age was an age of technological improvisation and desperation. A Dark Age blacksmith was not a proud innovator; he was a struggling artisan trying to make a usable tool from a difficult and unfamiliar material because he could no longer get the bronze he was used to working with. His first products were likely far inferior to the fine bronze tools of his ancestors. But they were something. Iron was the technology of self-sufficiency, a product of a world where you had to make do with what you could find locally because the global supply chain had collapsed. It was a technology born of necessity, a response to the great simplification. Over the centuries, as smiths perfected their techniques, iron would indeed become a superior metal, one that would arm new kinds of armies and reshape the world. But its origins lie in the poverty and isolation of the Dark Age.

The loss of interconnectedness was not just economic; it was cultural. The flow of ideas, artistic styles, and religious concepts that had cross-pollinated the Glimmering World came to a halt. The vibrant, cosmopolitan culture of port cities like Ugarit was replaced by a narrow, inward-looking parochialism. Each small region was on its own, its cultural development isolated from its neighbors. The world, which had been a great, interconnected sea, had evaporated, leaving behind a series of small, disconnected ponds.

Glimmers in the Darkness: The Stubborn Spark of Resilience

It would be easy to paint the Dark Age as a period of unmitigated gloom, a four-hundred-year-long winter of the human spirit. But that would be to miss the most important part of the story: the extraordinary resilience of the survivors. Collapse is a filter. It destroys the complex, top-heavy structures of society, but it does not always destroy the people. And in the wreckage, new, more flexible and adaptable forms of life begin to emerge.

The first sign of resilience is simple survival. The population of Greece may have plummeted, but people did not disappear. They adapted. The archaeological evidence for this is fascinating. In the ruins of the great citadel of Tiryns, in the decades after its destruction, we find evidence of squatters. People moved back into the burned-out shells of the palace buildings, clearing small areas of rubble, patching up walls with crude fieldstones, and building simple hearths on the floors where kings once held court. It is a powerful image: ordinary families making a home in the ruins of a world they could no longer build, but whose massive, protective stones could still offer some shelter.

In Athens, the story is one of continuity. The Acropolis, unlike the other Mycenaean centers, was never completely abandoned. It seems to have survived the worst of the destruction, providing a nucleus of continuous settlement that allowed Athens to weather the Dark Age better than its rivals, a fact that would have profound consequences for its later rise to prominence.

The second sign of resilience was adaptation. Farmers learned to work more marginal land. Herding became more important than settled agriculture, as animals could be moved more easily in times of trouble. People rediscovered old, local traditions that had been suppressed or overshadowed by the homogenous culture of the palaces. The Dark Age was not just an age of loss; it was an age of rediscovery and improvisation.

The third and most powerful form of resilience was memory, embodied in the oral tradition of the bards. As we have seen, the stories of the heroic age became a form of cultural glue, a way for scattered and impoverished communities to maintain a sense of a shared, glorious past. This was not just nostalgia. It was a creative act. By keeping the memory of the heroes alive, they were preserving the raw material from which a new Greek identity would be forged. The darkness was not a void; it was a period of gestation.

Finally, there was the slow, painful, but ultimately revolutionary embrace of new technologies and new social structures. The adoption of iron, born of necessity, would eventually arm a new kind of citizen-soldier, the hoplite, whose power lay not in an expensive, elite chariot, but in the collective strength of the phalanx. The collapse of the rigid, top-down palace system created a power vacuum that allowed for political experimentation. In the small, self-governing villages of the Dark Age, the seeds of a new and radical idea were planted: the idea of the *polis*, the self-governing city-state, where citizens, not kings, would hold power.

The long shadow of the Bronze Age, then, was both a curse and a blessing. It was a period of profound trauma, poverty, and loss. The world had been irrevocably broken. But the collapse also acted as a great, brutal pruning, clearing away the old, rigid, and brittle structures of the palace civilizations. It shattered the gilded cage of the Bronze Age world, and in doing so, it created the space for something new to grow.

The survivors who huddled in the ruins of Mycenae did not know what the future held. They knew only that the world of their ancestors was gone. But in their poverty, their isolation, and their struggle, they were, without knowing it, laying the foundations for a new world. The next chapters of our story belong to them and to their counterparts across the shattered landscape of the Near East. We will see how the defeated Peleset raiders used their Aegean heritage to build a powerful new nation in Canaan, and how the surviving Canaanite merchants of cities like Tyre and Sidon would reinvent trade and, in the process, give the world the transformative gift of the alphabet. The long, dark night was ending. A new, and very different, dawn was about to break.

13

The Raiders Settle Down: The Philistines

History is written by the victors. This is a truism we have seen demonstrated in the glorious, self-serving inscriptions of Ramesses III. He met the great confederation of the Sea Peoples in a cataclysm of fire and water, and he crushed them. He saved Egypt, broke the back of the invasion, and scattered its remnants. According to the logic of his own story, the threat was neutralized, the forces of chaos vanquished. The Sea Peoples were a footnote, a defeated rabble destined to disappear into the margins of history.

But history is more complex and far more interesting than the boasts of any pharaoh. For one of the key members of that defeated confederation, the story did not end in the bloody waters of the Nile Delta. For the Peleset, the warriors with the distinctive feathered headdresses, their defeat by Ramesses was not an ending. It was a beginning. It was the brutal, violent birth of a new nation.

This is the remarkable story of how a group of defeated sea-raiders and migrants transformed themselves into one of the most powerful and sophisticated peoples of the Iron Age. It is the story of how the Peleset settled on the southern coast of Canaan and became the Philistines of the Hebrew Bible—the great antagonists of Samson, Saul, and David. This is a chapter about what happens *after* the collapse, a powerful testament to the resilience and adaptability of the survivors.

By combining the biased accounts of their enemies—the Egyptians and the Israelites—with the silent but eloquent testimony of archaeology, we can reconstruct the world of the Philistines. We can walk the streets of their newly founded cities, examine the unique pottery they crafted, taste the food they ate, and understand how these former refugees built a vibrant and powerful state that would dominate the region for centuries. The story of the Philistines is the story of the sea-raiders settling down, and in doing so, forever changing the course of history in the land that would one day be called Palestine, a name derived from their own.

From Defeat to Dominion: The Egyptian Connection

How did a defeated people end up as the rulers of a new territory? The answer lies in the canny statecraft of their conqueror. Ramesses III had won a great victory, but he still had a problem. He had captured thousands of Peleset and Sherden warriors and their families. What was he to do with them? Enslaving such a large and warlike population was risky. Executing them all was impractical. So, Ramesses did what pragmatic rulers have always done with defeated but capable enemies: he co-opted them.

He settled them as garrison troops in a series of fortified towns along the southern coastal plain of Canaan. This was a strategic masterstroke. This region, known as the Shephelah, was a vital buffer zone, the gateway to Egypt from Asia. It had long been under Egyptian imperial control, but that control was slipping in the chaotic aftermath of the Bronze Age Collapse. The old Canaanite city-states that had once been loyal Egyptian vassals were weakened or destroyed.

By settling the Peleset and other Sea Peoples in this region, Ramesses achieved several goals at once. He removed a dangerous, concentrated group of warriors from Egypt itself. He created a loyal buffer state, a military colony of warrior-farmers who owed their new homes directly to him. Their job was to guard the Egyptian frontier against incursions from the hill country of Canaan and the deserts to the east. They were, in effect, hired as the border guards of the Egyptian empire, their settlement a form of payment for their service.

The Peleset, for their part, seized the opportunity. They had failed to conquer Egypt, but they had been granted the next best thing: a fertile new land to call their own. They settled in and around five major Canaanite cities, destroying what was left of the old structures and building new, fortified centers on top of the ruins. These five cities would become the famous Philistine Pentapolis: Ashdod, Ashkelon, and Gaza on the coast, and Ekron and Gath further inland. This was the birth of Philistia.

For a generation or two, the system worked. The Philistines served as Egyptian vassals, and Egyptian-style artifacts are found in the earliest levels of their settlements. But the Egyptian empire itself was in a state of terminal decline. The internal problems we saw in the Deir el-Medina strikes—economic chaos, corruption, and a loss of central authority—were crippling the state. By the middle of the 12th century B.C., Egypt's control over Canaan had evaporated. They withdrew their garrisons and abandoned their imperial ambitions in Asia forever.

The Philistines were now on their own. But they were not weak. They had a prime piece of real estate, controlling the fertile coastal plain and the lucrative international coastal highway. They had a strong military tradition. And they had a cohesive cultural identity. They rapidly consolidated their power, transforming from a collection of Egyptian garrison towns into a powerful, independent confederation of city-states that would come to dominate the entire region. The former mercenaries had become masters.

Digging for Goliath: The World of the Philistine Cities

For centuries, our only picture of the Philistines came from the pages of the Hebrew Bible. And it was not a flattering portrait. In the books of Judges and Samuel, they are the arch-enemies, the oppressive, uncircumcised idolaters who constantly threaten the fledgling nation of Israel. They are personified by the brutish giant Goliath, a champion of brute force and pagan arrogance. The word "philistine" has entered our own language as a term for an uncultured, boorish person.

But archaeology, over the last half-century, has given the Philistines a voice of their own. Extensive excavations at the sites of the Pentapolis cities, particularly at Ashdod, Ashkelon, and especially Ekron, have revealed a culture that was anything but boorish and uncultured. They have uncovered a people with a unique and sophisticated material culture, a vibrant economy, and a complex religious life—a culture that was a fascinating hybrid of their Aegean origins and their new Levantine surroundings.

Let us take a tour of Tel Miqne, the site of the ancient city of Ekron, one of the most thoroughly excavated Philistine sites. In the middle of the 12th century B.C., after the destruction of the old Canaanite city, a massive new city arises. It is well-planned and heavily fortified, with a thick mud-brick wall. The architecture is distinctive. Instead of the typical Canaanite courtyard houses, the early Philistine houses are built around a central hearth, a feature typical of Aegean and Cypriot domestic architecture. It is a small but powerful echo of the homes they left behind.

The most dramatic evidence of their foreign origin comes from their pottery. The earliest Philistine layers are filled with a type of pottery that archaeologists call Mycenaean IIIC:1b. This is a locally made but stylistically foreign pottery that is almost identical to the pottery being produced in Cyprus and the Aegean in the immediate aftermath of the Mycenaean collapse. It is as if a group of Mycenaean potters had packed up their wheels and their design books and moved to Canaan. This pottery includes distinctive shapes like bell-shaped craters and stirrup jars, decorated with stylized birds, fish, and geometric patterns. This is the calling card of the Sea Peoples, the tangible link that connects the Philistines of Canaan to the collapsing world of the Aegean.

As the decades passed, this pottery style evolved, blending with local Canaanite traditions to create the unique and elegant Philistine Bichrome ware, decorated in red and black paint. The bird motif remains, a persistent memory of their overseas origins. This ceramic evolution is a perfect metaphor for the Philistines themselves: they were a people who remembered where they came from, but who successfully adapted to their new environment.

The Philistines were not just potters and builders; they were master industrialists. The excavations at Ekron have uncovered the largest olive oil production center in the ancient Near East. In the 7th century B.C., the city had over one hundred olive oil presses. This was not for local consumption. This was a massive industrial enterprise, producing thousands of gallons of oil for export to Egypt and Assyria. The Philistines had taken control of a key agricultural industry and turned it into the engine of a thriving international trade economy.

They were also skilled metalworkers. While they did not introduce iron to the region, they seem to have quickly mastered its production, establishing an early dominance in iron weaponry that gave them a significant military advantage over their neighbors. The biblical story of how the Israelites had to go down to Philistine territory to have their iron tools sharpened (1 Samuel 13:19-21) is likely a reflection of this early Philistine technological superiority.

Gods and Feasting: A Glimpse into Philistine Culture

What did the Philistines believe? The Bible portrays them as idol-worshippers, their chief god being Dagon, a Canaanite deity of grain. Archaeology reveals a more complex picture. In the early years of their settlement, their religion seems to have been a direct transplant from the Aegean. Excavations have uncovered small, terracotta figurines of seated goddesses, their hands raised in a gesture of mourning or blessing. These are almost identical to the so-called "Mourning Goddess" figurines found at Mycenae and other late Bronze Age sites in Greece. They seem to have brought their own goddesses with them.

Over time, however, they adopted many of the local Canaanite deities, including Dagon and Baal. Their religion, like their pottery, became a hybrid. A remarkable discovery at Ekron brought this vividly to life. In the ruins of a massive temple complex dating to the 7th century B.C., archaeologists found a monumental limestone inscription. It is a royal dedicatory inscription, naming the king who built the temple, a man named Ikausu (a non-Semitic name, possibly derived from "Achaean" or Greek), and it dedicates the temple to a goddess. The inscription calls her *Ptgyh*, a previously unknown deity. But who was she? The inscription refers to her as Ikausu's "lady." Some scholars speculate that *Ptgyh* could be a Philistine rendering of *Potnia*, the ancient Greek word for "Mistress" or "Lady," a common title for Mycenaean goddesses. If so, it is a stunning example of cultural memory, the name of an ancestral Aegean goddess surviving for five hundred years in a new land.

The Philistines also had a distinctive diet. Analysis of animal bones from their settlements shows a surprisingly high percentage of pig bones, especially in the early phases of their settlement. This is in stark contrast to their Canaanite and Israelite neighbors, for whom pork was a dietary taboo. They also consumed a significant amount of beef and dog meat. This unique "dietary signature" is another powerful marker of their foreign identity. They brought their culinary traditions, as well as their gods and potters, with them from the West.

Their social and political structure also seems to have been unique. The Pentapolis was not a unified kingdom, but a confederation of five independent city-states, each ruled by a leader known in the Hebrew Bible by the title *seren*. This word is not Semitic, and scholars have long noted its similarity to the Greek word *tyrannos* (tyrant), which in its earliest usage simply meant a lord or ruler. It is likely that the Philistine political system, a league of allied cities, was another import from their Aegean past.

The Israelite Rivalry: A Clash of Cultures

As the Philistines consolidated their power on the coastal plain, they inevitably came into conflict with the other major group that was coalescing in the region during the Iron Age: the Israelites, who were settling the central hill country. The famous stories of the Bible—Samson and Delilah, the capture of the Ark of the Covenant, David and Goliath—are the national epic of the Israelites, but they are also a testament to the power and influence of the Philistines.

This was more than just a military conflict. It was a clash of two very different cultures. The Philistines were a cosmopolitan, urban, and technologically advanced people with deep roots in the international world of the Mediterranean. The early Israelites were a more rural, tribal, and inward-looking society, their identity forged in the rugged hill country. The Philistines controlled the fertile plains and the trade routes; the Israelites controlled the less desirable highlands.

For over a century, the Philistines had the upper hand. Their superior military organization and iron weaponry allowed them to dominate their Israelite neighbors, often demanding tribute and restricting their access to technology. The story of Goliath, stripped of its miraculous ending, is a perfect allegory for the conflict. Goliath is a champion of the old way of war. He is a heavily armored warrior, a walking tank, covered in bronze and iron, challenging the enemy to a formal, one-on-one duel. He represents the organized, professional military power of the Philistine city-states. David, the shepherd boy with a simple sling, represents the guerrilla tactics and unconventional warfare of the highland tribes.

The eventual rise of the Israelite monarchy under Saul and then David was a direct response to the Philistine threat. The Israelites realized that to compete with the highly organized Philistine confederation, they needed to abandon their loose tribal structure and create a centralized state of their own. The creation of the Kingdom of Israel was, in many ways, an act of political mimesis, an attempt to build a state capable of standing up to the powerful Philistine model.

In the end, under the leadership of King David, the Israelites managed to break the back of Philistine dominance, pushing them back to their coastal strongholds. But the Philistines were never conquered. They remained a powerful and independent force in the region for another four hundred years, until they, like the kingdoms of Israel and Judah, were finally absorbed into the great Iron Age empires of Assyria and Babylonia.

The Legacy of the Raiders

The story of the Philistines is a powerful counter-narrative to the simple story of collapse and decay. It demonstrates that the end of one world is often the beginning of another. The Peleset, who appear on the walls of Medinet Habu as part of a defeated, chaotic mob, did not simply vanish. They survived, they adapted, and they thrived.

They are a testament to the incredible power of cultural resilience. They carried the memory of their Aegean homeland with them across the sea—in the style of their pottery, the architecture of their homes, the names of their gods, and the food they ate. But they were not slavish imitators of their past. They were brilliant innovators, blending their ancestral traditions with the new realities of their Levantine home to create a unique and dynamic hybrid culture. They transformed themselves from landless sea-raiders into master merchants, industrialists, and state-builders.

Their legacy is written across the land. They gave their name to the region that would forever after be known as Palestine. They were the catalyst that forced the tribes of Israel to forge a unified kingdom. And they stand as the most vivid and well-documented example of what happened to the Sea Peoples after the great wave of destruction had passed.

The defeated warriors of Ramesses III's reliefs, the desperate refugees in their oxcarts, did not just fade into the darkness. They stepped out of the shadow of collapse and, in a remarkable act of historical reinvention, built a new world for themselves on the ashes of the old. They prove that even in the midst of a dark age, the human capacity for creation is not so easily extinguished.

14

The God from the Mountains

In the ashes of the Bronze Age, new societies began to form, each a unique experiment in survival and reinvention. On the fertile coastal plain, the Philistines built their powerful city-states, a vibrant hybrid of their Aegean past and their Levantine present. They built temples to their ancestral goddesses and to the great gods of Canaan, Dagon and Baal. Their world was a continuation, an adaptation of the cosmopolitan, polytheistic tapestry of the Glimmering World.

But in the rugged, limestone hills to their east, in the highlands that rose from the Shephelah, a different kind of revolution was taking place. A collection of scattered, rural, tribal communities—the people who would become Israel—were coalescing around a radical and unprecedented idea. It was an idea that was as much a product of the collapse as iron smelting or the alphabet, but one that would prove infinitely more influential. They were beginning to forge a relationship with a single, jealous, and terrifyingly powerful God.

This was the birth of Yahweh. Not the universal, transcendent, and singular God of later Judaism, Christianity, and Islam, but the embryonic form of that God: a fierce and warlike deity of the mountains and the storm, a divine patron who demanded absolute and exclusive loyalty in a world teeming with other gods. The story of Yahweh's rise from an obscure desert storm god to the sole creator of the universe is one of the most remarkable theological journeys in human history. It is a story of syncretism, rivalry, and revolution.

The emergence of monotheism was not a gentle philosophical revelation. It was a messy, centuries-long political and religious struggle, forged in the crucible of the Iron Age. It was a direct reaction against the old, interconnected world of the Bronze Age, with its shared pantheons and easy religious borrowing. The idea of a single, universal God would have been unthinkable in the cosmopolitan court of Ugarit or the imperial center of Hattusa. The collapse of that world, the great simplification and fragmentation, created the space for this new, exclusive, and portable idea of God to take root. To understand the world that emerged from the ashes, we must understand the origins of the God who would come to define it.

The Divine Family Reunion: The World of Canaanite Gods

Before Yahweh, there was the family. The religious landscape of the Bronze Age Levant, the world into which both the Philistines and Israelites arrived, was dominated by a rich and complex pantheon of gods whose stories are best preserved in the epic poems discovered in the ruins of Ugarit. To understand the revolution Yahweh represented, we must first meet the divine establishment he would ultimately overthrow.

At the head of this divine family was **El**. El was the patriarch, the ancient and wise father of the gods. He was the ultimate creator, the source of all things. In the Ugaritic texts, he is depicted as a remote, venerable figure, a gray-bearded king who dwells at the "source of the two rivers," the mythological center of the universe. He is benevolent, wise, and powerful, but also somewhat distant from the day-to-day affairs of gods and mortals. He is the chairman of the board, presiding over the divine assembly where the fates are decided. His consort is the great mother goddess, **Asherah**, "She Who Treads on the Sea."

But the star of the show, the most active and important god in the pantheon, was **Baal**. His name simply means "Lord," and his proper name was Hadad. Baal was the young, virile, and ambitious god of the storm. He was the god of the life-giving winter rains, the one whose thunderous voice echoed in the mountains and whose lightning split the sky. His power was immediate and vital. While El was the creator, Baal was the sustainer, the divine warrior who fought the forces of chaos to ensure the fertility of the land.

The great epic of Ugarit, the Baal Cycle, is a dramatic story of his struggles. It tells of his titanic battle against **Yam**, the chaotic god of the sea, a story that echoes the Mesopotamian myth of Marduk and Tiamat. Baal, with the help of magical weapons forged by the divine craftsman Kothar-wa-Khasis, defeats Yam and is crowned king of the gods. He then battles **Mot**, the god of death and sterility, who rules the arid underworld. In a dramatic cycle that mirrors the changing seasons, Baal is swallowed by Mot and descends to the underworld (representing the dry summer season), only to be rescued and resurrected, his return bringing the rains and new life to the land.

This was the religious world of Canaan. It was a nature-based religion, its central drama reflecting the annual cycle of rain and drought, life and death. The pantheon was a complex family, full of rivalries, alliances, and dramatic stories. A farmer in Canaan would have worshipped Baal for rain, Dagon for the grain, Asherah for fertility, and looked to the great father El as the ultimate authority. It was a rich, polytheistic system, perfectly adapted to its agricultural environment. This was the family that Yahweh was about to crash.

The God Who Came from the South

So, where did Yahweh come from? He does not appear in the Ugaritic pantheon. He is absent from the religious texts of Mesopotamia and Anatolia. The archaeological and textual evidence points to a surprising and specific origin: Yahweh was not a native of Canaan. He was an import from the south, a god of the desert wilderness.

Our first extra-biblical clues come not from Canaan, but from Egypt. Inscriptions from the reigns of the New Kingdom pharaohs Amenhotep III and Ramesses II, found at Soleb and Amara West in Nubia (modern-day Sudan), list the various nomadic tribes, or *Shasu*, whom the Egyptians encountered on their southern and eastern frontiers. One of these groups is identified as the "Shasu-land of YHW." YHW is a perfectly plausible Egyptian rendering of the name Yahweh. This suggests that as early as the 14th century B.C., the Egyptians knew of a specific group of nomadic peoples in the deserts south of Canaan who worshipped a god named Yahweh.

This aligns perfectly with some of the oldest traditions within the Hebrew Bible itself. The earliest poems in the Bible, like the Song of Deborah in Judges 5 and the Blessing of Moses in Deuteronomy 33, consistently describe Yahweh as coming from the south.

"Yahweh, when you went out from Seir, when you marched from the region of Edom, the earth trembled, the heavens also dripped..." (Judges 5:4)

"Yahweh came from Sinai, and dawned on them from Seir; He shone forth from Mount Paran..." (Deuteronomy 33:2)

Seir, Edom, Sinai, Paran—all of these are locations in the arid, mountainous desert regions to the south of Judah. The Bible's own memory preserves the tradition that Yahweh was not originally from the hills of Ephraim or Judah, but was a god of the southern wilderness, a god of the mountain and the storm, whose home was a place of fire and trembling earth.

This has led to what is known as the **Kenite Hypothesis**. This theory proposes that the worship of Yahweh was introduced to the early Israelites by a group of Midianite or Kenite metalworkers. The Bible itself contains intriguing hints of this connection. Moses's father-in-law is described as a priest of Midian, and it is at a burning bush on a sacred mountain in Midian (Horeb/Sinai) that Yahweh first reveals his name to Moses. The Kenites were a clan of itinerant metalworkers, and it is fascinating to speculate that these smiths, who controlled the powerful and almost magical technology of metallurgy, may have had a powerful, fiery god as their patron deity—a god of the volcano and the forge.

Whether through the Kenites or other channels, it seems clear that a group of early proto-Israelites, perhaps the "Moses group" that the Bible describes as escaping from Egypt, encountered the cult of this powerful southern storm god and adopted him as their own. When they began to settle in the highlands of Canaan, they brought their fierce, desert god with them, introducing him into the complex and crowded world of the Canaanite pantheon.

The Great Merger: Yahweh vs. Baal and El

The arrival of Yahweh in Canaan set the stage for a divine showdown. The early Israelites, settling down as farmers, were now living in Baal's territory. Baal was the established god of the rain, the lord of the fertile land. It was only natural that many Israelites would be drawn to his worship. The land belonged to Baal, and to ensure good crops, one had to placate him.

This created a profound religious tension, a rivalry that would dominate Israelite religion for centuries. The prophets of Yahweh saw the worship of Baal as an act of apostasy, a betrayal of their covenant with their own divine patron. The Hebrew Bible is filled with furious polemics against Baal worship. The most famous of these is the dramatic story of the prophet Elijah's contest with the prophets of Baal on Mount Carmel (1 Kings 18).

In the story, Elijah challenges 450 prophets of Baal to a contest to see whose god will answer with fire from heaven. The prophets of Baal dance and shout and even cut themselves, but "there was no voice, no one answered, no one paid attention." Then Elijah, after dousing his own altar with water, calls on Yahweh, and fire flashes down from heaven, consuming the sacrifice. The story is a piece of brilliant theological propaganda. It is a direct assault on Baal's authority, showing that Yahweh, not Baal, is the true master of fire and the elements.

But the relationship was not just one of rivalry; it was also one of absorption. Over time, Yahweh began to take on the characteristics of his great rival. Like Baal, Yahweh becomes the divine warrior who rides on the clouds. Like Baal, he is the storm god whose voice is thunder. And like Baal, he is the one who battles the forces of chaos, personified by the sea and the great sea monster, Leviathan.

In Psalm 74, the psalmist praises Yahweh in terms that could have been lifted directly from the Ugaritic Baal Cycle: "You divided the sea by your might; you broke the heads of the dragons in the waters. You crushed the heads of Leviathan…" Yahweh was effectively supplanting Baal, taking over his job description and his epic stories.

At the same time, Yahweh was also merging with the great father god, El. The name "Israel" itself likely means "El struggles" or "El rules." The early patriarchs, Abraham, Isaac, and Jacob, are described as worshipping God under names like *El Shaddai* (God of the Mountain/Almighty), *El Elyon* (God Most High), and *El Olam* (The Eternal God). These are all titles of the Canaanite high god, El.

As the Yahweh cult grew in prominence, it absorbed these El traditions. Yahweh took on El's role as the creator of the world, the father of his people, and the wise, presiding head of the divine council. The phrase "assembly of the holy ones" or "council of the gods" appears in the Psalms, a direct echo of the divine assembly presided over by El in the Ugaritic texts. In one remarkable passage (Psalm 82), Yahweh is depicted as standing up in the middle of the divine assembly and condemning the other gods for their unjust rule, effectively staging a divine coup and taking over the leadership from El.

This double-merger was a theological masterstroke. Yahweh acquired the storm-god power and agricultural relevance of Baal, and the primordial, creative authority of El. He became a super-god, a deity who combined the most powerful attributes of his chief rivals. He was now both the transcendent creator and the immanent, active storm god, a figure of unparalleled power and scope.

From One God Among Many to the Only God

This process of absorption and suppression still took place within a polytheistic framework. For most of its early history, the religion of Israel was not monotheistic. It was **monolatrous**. Monolatry is the belief in the existence of many gods, but the consistent worship of only one of them. The First Commandment is the classic statement of monolatry: "You shall have no other gods *before me*" (or *besides me*). The commandment does not deny the existence of Chemosh, the god of the Moabites, or Milcom, the god of the Ammonites. It simply forbids an Israelite from worshipping them.

This was a religion of fierce, exclusive loyalty to a divine patron. Yahweh was *our* god, and we are *his* people. He was a jealous god who would not tolerate his followers "whoring after" other deities. This idea of a covenant, a binding, exclusive contract between a people and their patron god, was the core of early Israelite identity. It was a powerful social glue, a way of maintaining a distinct cultural identity in a world of powerful, assimilating neighbors like the Philistines.

The archaeological evidence supports this picture of a complex religious landscape. Small female figurines, likely representing the mother goddess Asherah, are found in abundance in Israelite households all the way through the monarchic period. This suggests that, despite the official, Yahweh-centric religion promoted by the prophets and the Jerusalem priesthood, many ordinary Israelites continued to worship other deities, particularly Asherah as Yahweh's consort. The struggle for the heart and soul of Israel was a long and difficult one.

The final, radical leap from monolatry to true **monotheism**—the belief that only one God exists at all—seems to have been crystallized by a national catastrophe: the Babylonian Exile. In 586 B.C., the Babylonian empire conquered the kingdom of Judah, destroyed the Temple of Solomon in Jerusalem (Yahweh's earthly home), and carried off the elite of the population into exile in Babylon.

This was a theological crisis of the first order. The traditional ancient Near Eastern view would be that the god of the Babylonians, Marduk, had proven himself stronger than Yahweh. Yahweh had been defeated, his temple destroyed, his people exiled. The logical conclusion was to abandon the loser and start worshipping the winner.

But a group of Judean prophets and thinkers, most notably the anonymous prophet known as Second Isaiah, performed a breathtaking act of theological reinterpretation. They argued the opposite. The destruction had not happened because Yahweh was weak. It had happened because Yahweh was powerful, and he had used the Babylonian empire as his *instrument* to punish his own people for their sin of worshipping other gods.

This required a radical new conception of God. Yahweh was not just the god of Israel; he was the God of the entire world, the one who controlled the destinies of all nations, including the mighty Babylonian empire. The other gods were not his rivals; they were nothing, mere idols of wood and stone.

"I am Yahweh, and there is no other; besides me there is no god," declares the prophet in Isaiah 45. "I form light and create darkness, I make well-being and create calamity; I am Yahweh, who does all these things."

This is the birth of true, exclusive, universal monotheism. It was an idea forged in the crucible of defeat and exile. It was a way of making sense of a national tragedy and preserving a cultural identity in a foreign land. The God of Israel could no longer be tied to a specific temple or a specific territory. He had to become a portable God, a universal God who could be worshipped anywhere, because he was the God of everywhere.

The Revolutionary God

The rise of Yahwism was one of the most significant consequences of the Bronze Age Collapse. The breakdown of the old, international, polytheistic world created the conditions for this new, exclusive, and revolutionary idea to emerge. In the stable, interconnected Glimmering World, a god like Yahweh would have likely been absorbed into the existing pantheon, becoming just another local storm god among many. But in the fragmented, chaotic, and competitive world of the Iron Age, his fierce demand for exclusive loyalty became a powerful tool for forging a unique national identity.

The story of Yahweh is the ultimate story of survival and adaptation from the ashes of the collapse. It was a theological innovation as radical and transformative as the alphabet. Like the Philistines, the Israelites built a new world for themselves after the great unraveling. But while the Philistines built their new world out of pottery, olive presses, and iron swords, the Israelites built theirs out of an idea—the idea of a single, universal God. It was an idea that would survive the fall of their own kingdom, that would be carried out of the ashes of their own temple, and that would go on to shape the spiritual and intellectual history of half the human race. The God who began as a fiery deity of a remote desert mountain had become the God of all creation. The long shadow of the Bronze Age was long indeed, and in its darkness, a new and powerful light had begun to shine.

15

Masters of the Alphabet: The Phoenician Dawn

The story of the Bronze Age Collapse, as we have told it, is a story of endings. It is a chronicle of fire and ruin, of great empires turned to dust and glittering palaces reduced to ash. It is a symphony of silent screams. The Hittites, a superpower that had challenged Egypt and sacked Babylon, vanished from their Anatolian homeland. The Mycenaeans, the heroes of Homer's epic songs, saw their mighty citadels consumed by flames, their culture shattered, and their knowledge of writing extinguished. The great cosmopolitan hub of Ugarit, the jewel of the Levant, sent one last, desperate letter before it was wiped from the face of the earth. The world had been broken.

But collapse is never a final word. It is a filter, a brutal and unforgiving process of natural selection for civilizations. In the most devastating forest fire, some ancient, deep-rooted trees always survive. Sheltered in a protected canyon, possessing a unique resilience in their bark, or simply lucky, they weather the inferno. And when the fire has passed, when the smoke has cleared and the ground is a blanket of sterile ash, it is their seeds, carried on the wind, that will repopulate the barren landscape.

On the coast of the Levant, in a narrow, fertile strip of land nestled between the formidable Lebanon mountain range and the Mediterranean Sea, a few such trees survived. While the great cities to their north and south were consumed, a handful of ancient Canaanite port cities—most notably Tyre, Sidon, Byblos, and Arwad—clung to life. They were damaged, certainly. They were diminished, their trade networks shattered, their political world turned upside down. But they were not destroyed. These survivors, the direct heirs of the Bronze Age Canaanite culture, would become the great innovators of the new age. They would rise from the ashes not as conquerors, but as explorers, merchants, and intellectual revolutionaries. History would know them by the name the Greeks gave them: the *Phoinikes*, the Phoenicians.

The story of the Phoenicians is the story of the ultimate pivot. They were the survivors who looked out at the wreckage of the Glimmering World and did not see an ending, but a beginning. They saw a power vacuum. The collapse of the great, centralized palace economies had swept the old masters from the board. The game was now open. The Phoenicians stepped into this void. They abandoned the rigid, top-down, royally-sponsored model of the past and invented a new way of doing business: a decentralized, flexible, and daringly entrepreneurial maritime trading network that was perfectly adapted to the chaotic, fragmented new world.

They became the new masters of the sea, their pennants recognized in every port from the Nile Delta to the stormy coast of Spain. They were the connectors, the middlemen, the human shuttles who would re-stitch the torn fabric of the Mediterranean world. And in the process of building their commercial empire, they would bestow upon the world a gift of incalculable value, a piece of intellectual technology so elegant and so powerful it would fundamentally reshape human consciousness. They perfected the alphabet. They took a principle that had been circulating in the Near East for centuries, refined it into a simple, beautiful system of twenty-two signs, and exported it along with their cedarwood and purple dye. This was the script that would allow the Greeks to write down their philosophy, the Romans to build their empire of law, and you, three thousand years later, to read these very words. The Phoenician dawn was not just the beginning of a new economic age; it was the beginning of a new age of the mind.

The Art of Survival

Why did Tyre and Sidon survive while Ugarit, just up the coast, perished? The question is central to understanding the Phoenician miracle. The answer appears to lie in a potent combination of geography, political shrewdness, and perhaps a healthy dose of luck.

First, geography provided a crucial defense. The city of Tyre, in its original and most powerful incarnation, was not on the mainland. It was an offshore island, a "rock" in the sea (its name, Ṣur, means "rock"), situated about half a mile from the coast. This made it a formidable fortress. A land-based army, no matter how large, was useless against it without a powerful navy to impose a blockade and mount an amphibious assault. A fleet of sea-raiders, on the other hand, would face a city whose entire population were master mariners, fighting in their home waters. This natural defensibility gave Tyre a security that cities like Ugarit, situated on the mainland, lacked. It was this island fortress that would famously resist the siege of the Babylonian king Nebuchadnezzar for thirteen years, and would only fall to Alexander the Great after he built a massive causeway to connect it to the shore.

But geography alone is not enough. The Phoenicians were, above all, pragmatists. They were merchants, not ideologues. Their primary goal was not conquest, but commerce. It is highly probable that their survival was due to a deliberate policy of accommodation. While other cities manned their walls and prepared for battle, the merchant-princes of Tyre and Sidon may have chosen a different path. Imagine a fleet of Sea Peoples ships, their bird-headed prows menacing, appearing off the coast of Tyre. The Tyrians, seeing this overwhelming force, might not have sent out warships. They might have sent out a diplomatic envoy with a simple, compelling offer: "What do you need? We have fresh water, grain, wine. We can repair your ships. We can trade our fine cloth for your captured metal. Let us do business."

By making themselves more valuable as a neutral port of call and a supply depot than as a target for plunder, they may have successfully deflected the main force of the migrations. They bent with the great storm, and so they did not break. This was the Phoenician genius: to see a potential enemy and find a way to turn them into a customer.

The *Story of Wenamun*, that priceless papyrus from the 11th century B.C., offers a perfect snapshot of the new political reality. The unfortunate Egyptian priest, Wenamun, arrives in the port of Byblos to procure cedar for a new sacred barge for the god Amun. In the old days of the empire, such a request would have been a command. The local prince of Byblos, as a loyal vassal, would have immediately complied. But the world has changed.

Wenamun is forced to wait on the beach for nearly a month before the prince, Zakar-Baal, will even grant him an audience. When they finally meet, the exchange is a study in Phoenician pride and Egyptian impotence. Wenamun makes a speech about the greatness of his god, Amun. Zakar-Baal retorts that his own ancestors fulfilled such orders, but only after the pharaoh had sent six ships laden with Egyptian goods as payment. He then delivers the killer lines that define the new age:

"I am not your servant! I am not the servant of him that sent you either! ... As for this sea, it is the sea of Amun? The sea belongs to me! And this Lebanon, it is his? The Lebanon belongs to me! And this fleet of mine, it belongs to Amun? It is mine!"

The prince of Byblos, a minor player in the old world, now sees himself as the master of his own domain, his power rooted in his control of the cedar trade and his personal fleet of merchant ships. The great land-based empire of Egypt has become irrelevant. The sea now belongs to the Phoenicians.

The Lean Startup: A New World, A New Business Model

The collapse of the Bronze Age palace economies was a cataclysm, but for the Phoenicians, it was also a liberation. The old system of trade was cumbersome, a top-down affair controlled by the whims of kings and the slow grinding of palace bureaucracies. A trading expedition was a massive state-sponsored enterprise, requiring royal approval, scribal oversight, and military escorts.

The Phoenicians, out of necessity and ingenuity, invented a new system. It was the ancient world's version of the lean startup: decentralized, privatized, flexible, and driven by individual initiative. The engine of the Phoenician economy was not the palace, but the family. Trade was dominated by powerful merchant families who owned their own ships, financed their own voyages, and built their own commercial networks based on kinship and trust.

Imagine a man named Hiram, a merchant of Tyre in the 10th century B.C. He does not work for the king. He is the head of a family firm, a business passed down from his father. His assets are his two ships, a warehouse near the harbor, and his web of contacts in Cyprus and the Aegean. He hears from a returning captain that there is a high demand for fine linen in a port on Crete, and that a local chieftain there is willing to trade raw copper at a good price. Hiram doesn't need to file a request with a royal bureaucracy. He consults with his brothers and sons, calculates the risks and potential profits, loads one of his ships with fine cloth from Sidon and Egyptian papyrus, hires a reliable captain and crew, and sends them off.

The ship itself, a sturdy *gaulos* with its rounded hull and deep hold, is a floating business venture. The captain has the autonomy to adapt. If the port on Crete is no longer welcoming, he can sail on to the next island. If he finds an unexpected opportunity to trade for ivory, he has the authority to make the deal. This flexibility was a massive competitive advantage in the fragmented and unpredictable Iron Age.

This new model fostered a different kind of culture. It was a culture that valued risk-taking, entrepreneurship, and practical knowledge. A successful Phoenician merchant needed to be a skilled navigator, a savvy negotiator, a multilingual communicator, and a keen observer of market trends. This was a far cry from the life of a palace scribe, whose primary skill was the meticulous recording of inventories. The Phoenicians were creating a new kind of man: the international businessman.

The Wares of a Global Network

With their new business model and their sturdy ships, the Phoenicians became the indispensable carriers of the new age. They reconnected the shattered world, and their main export was their own ingenuity.

Their most famous and lucrative product, of course, was Tyrian purple. The secret of this dye was the foundation of Tyre's legendary wealth. The process was both an art and a science, and a thoroughly disgusting one at that. Fishermen would harvest two species of sea snail, *Bolinus brandaris* and *Hexaplex trunculus*, from the coastal waters. In workshops near the shore, the snails' glands were extracted and left to steep in vats of stale urine and salt water. The mixture was then heated and allowed to putrefy for several days under the sun. The smell would have been indescribable, a pungent mix of rotting seafood and ammonia that would have permeated the entire city. But the result was magical. The chemical reaction produced a dye of unparalleled brilliance and permanence, a range of hues from deep violet to crimson. To produce a single ounce of dye required tens of thousands of snails. The cost was astronomical. Only kings, high priests, and the fabulously wealthy could afford to wear true purple. It was the ultimate status symbol, and the Phoenicians had a monopoly on it. The great mounds of discarded Murex shells found by archaeologists around Tyre and Sidon are the silent monuments to this ancient chemical industry.

Another key export was **cedarwood**. The magnificent cedars of the Lebanon mountains were legendary throughout the ancient world. Their strong, aromatic, and rot-resistant timber was the preferred material for building temples, palaces, and high-status ships. The Epic of Gilgamesh speaks of the hero traveling to the Cedar Forest to battle the monster Humbaba. The Egyptians, with their wood-poor land, had been importing Lebanese cedar for millennia. The Phoenicians now controlled this priceless resource. The Bible records in great detail how King Solomon of Israel entered into a major trade agreement with King Hiram of Tyre to procure the vast quantities of cedar and cypress wood needed to build the First Temple in Jerusalem. In exchange, Solomon provided Hiram with wheat and olive oil, a classic exchange between the agricultural highlands and the commercial coast.

Beyond their own natural resources, the Phoenicians were

master craftsmen. Their skill in **ivory carving** was unparalleled. They would import raw elephant tusks from Africa via Egypt and transform them into exquisite luxury items: decorative plaques for furniture, cosmetic boxes, and ornate handles. The so-called "Nimrud Ivories," a spectacular hoard of Phoenician carvings discovered in the ruins of the Assyrian capital of Nimrud, showcase their artistry. The style is a fascinating and deliberate fusion of Egyptian, Syrian, and Mesopotamian motifs, perfectly tailored for their international clientele. They carved sphinxes in the Egyptian style, griffins in the Aegean style, and scenes of tribute that would appeal to Assyrian kings. They were not just artists; they were brilliant marketers, creating products with global appeal.

The same was true of their **metalwork**. They produced beautiful bronze and silver bowls, often decorated with intricate chased and repoussé scenes. These bowls have been found all over the Mediterranean, from Etruscan tombs in Italy to the sacred precinct at Olympia in Greece, a testament to their wide distribution and high value.

Beyond the Pillars of Hercules

The Phoenician thirst for new markets and new sources of raw materials drove them on voyages of exploration that would have been unimaginable to the Bronze Age palace kings. Their great leap forward was the push into the Western Mediterranean and beyond. They were drawn west by the lure of metal. The Iberian Peninsula (modern Spain and Portugal) was the El Dorado of the ancient world, fabulously rich in silver, copper, and tin.

To reach these resources, the Phoenicians established their characteristic chain of trading colonies. These were not colonies of conquest, but commercial footholds, a string of pearls along the great sea routes. They founded settlements in Cyprus, Sicily, Malta, and Sardinia. And then they took the great leap. They sailed past the Strait of Gibraltar, the place the Greeks called the Pillars of Hercules, a terrifying threshold that marked the end of the known world. To sail beyond it was to enter the vast, unknown, and terrifying Atlantic Ocean.

The Phoenicians did it. On the Atlantic coast of Spain, they founded the city of Gadir (modern Cádiz), a thriving port that would channel the mineral wealth of Iberia back into the Mediterranean. From here, their most daring sailors may have ventured even further. The Greek historian Herodotus reports, with some skepticism, that Phoenician mariners, commissioned by the Egyptian Pharaoh Necho II in the 6th century B.C., successfully circumnavigated Africa, a journey that would not be repeated for two thousand years. While the claim is debated, it speaks to their reputation as the most fearless and capable sailors of their time. Their navigational skills were legendary. They were the first to master the art of sailing at night, navigating not by hugging the coast, but by steering by the stars, particularly the North Star. The Greeks, in fact, often referred to the North Star as the *Phoinike*, the "Phoenician Star," in honor of the people who had taught them how to use it.

The most famous of all their colonial ventures was the city of Carthage, founded on the coast of Tunisia in the late 9th century B.C. The Roman legend of its founding tells of the Tyrian princess Dido, who fled the political turmoil of her home city and tricked a local Berber king into giving her as much land as could be covered by an oxhide. She then cleverly cut the hide into a single, continuous thin strip, enclosing a large enough area to found her "New City," *Qart Hadasht*. While the story is a myth, it captures the essence of the Phoenician method: expansion through cunning and commerce, not brute force. Carthage would eventually grow to become a great empire in its own right, its power and wealth so vast that it would take the rising Roman Republic three epic and bloody Punic Wars to finally destroy it.

The Alphabet: A Technology for a New World

For all their material accomplishments, the Phoenicians' most world-changing innovation was a technology of the mind. It was the perfection and dissemination of the alphabet.

The Bronze Age scripts—cuneiform and hieroglyphics—were beautiful, complex, and deeply inefficient. They were the tools of a scribal elite, requiring years of study to master. They were suited for the slow, monumental, and centralized world of the palaces. The Phoenicians, with their fast-paced, decentralized, and commercial culture, needed something better. They needed a script that was as lean and efficient as their business model.

They found the answer in the alphabetic principle that had been floating around the Levant for centuries. They took this idea and streamlined it into a system of unparalleled elegance: twenty-two simple, linear signs, each representing a single consonant. The entire system could be written down quickly and learned in a fraction of the time required for the old scripts.

The alphabet was a disruptive technology. It democratized literacy. It took the power of the written word out of the exclusive hands of the palace and temple scribes and gave it to the merchant, the artisan, and the sailor. It was a tool perfectly designed for a world of contracts, bills of lading, personal letters, and private accounts. It was the engine of a commercial revolution.

As the Phoenician traders established their colonies and trading posts across the Mediterranean, they carried their alphabet with them. In the ports of the Aegean, the Greeks, just beginning to emerge from their 400-year Dark Age, encountered this revolutionary new tool. Sometime in the 9th or 8th century B.C., they borrowed the Phoenician script. But they added a stroke of genius. The Phoenician alphabet, like other Semitic scripts, represented only consonants. The Greeks took several of the Phoenician signs for which they had no corresponding sound (like the glottal stop *'aleph* and the pharyngeal sound *'ayin*) and repurposed them to represent vowel sounds (*alpha, e psilon, omicron*).

This final innovation created the world's first complete phonetic alphabet, a system that could represent the full range of spoken sound. This Greek alphabet was a technology of breathtaking analytical power. It made it possible to transcribe complex philosophical arguments, to record nuanced poetry, and to write down detailed historical narratives with unprecedented accuracy. It was the tool that would enable the intellectual explosion of Classical Greece. The Romans would later adopt this alphabet from the Greeks via the Etruscans, and it is this Latin alphabet that has become the most widely used script in the world today.

The line of descent is direct and unbroken. The 'A' you are reading now began its life as the Phoenician letter *aleph*, which itself was derived from a proto-Sinaitic hieroglyph of an ox's head. The 'B' comes from *bet*, the Phoenician word for "house." Every time we write, we are unconsciously summoning the ghosts of these ancient Canaanite merchants.

The Phoenix Rises

The Phoenicians were the great unsung heroes of the post-collapse world. They were not conquerors who built a great territorial empire. Their legacy is not found in massive ruins or epic war poems. Their empire was a fluid network of ships and ideas. They were the connectors, the pragmatists, the innovators who saw a world in ruins and chose to build bridges rather than walls.

They inherited a world that was fragmented, impoverished, and isolated. They left it reconnected, revitalized, and equipped with the single most powerful tool for communication ever invented. They were the masters of the new dawn, the people who proved that the end of one age is always the prelude to the next. The Glimmering World of the Bronze Age was dead, but the seeds it had planted, carried on the sturdy ships of the Phoenician merchants, were about to blossom into the entirely new and brilliant world of classical antiquity. The phoenix had truly risen from the ashes.

Conclusion

We began our journey with a crime scene: a glittering, globalized world lying in ruins, and a mysterious suspect, the Sea Peoples, standing over the body. For three thousand years, they have been the primary culprits, the barbarian horde, the phantom menace responsible for the single greatest societal collapse in human history. We set out to investigate this ancient cold case, to sift through the evidence, to listen to the testimony of the dead, and to deliver a final verdict.

That verdict is now clear. The Late Bronze Age was not murdered by a single assassin. Its death was not a simple case of foreign invasion. It was a systems collapse. It was the death of a world from a thousand cuts, a perfect storm of converging crises that overwhelmed its defenses and shattered its very foundations. The Sea Peoples were not the killers. They were the coroners, the ones who arrived to officially pronounce the death of a civilization that was already lying on its deathbed.

The true culprits were forces far more fundamental, and far more familiar to our own age.

First, there was climate change. A sudden, severe, and prolonged megadrought, documented in the silent archives of lakebeds and ice cores, struck the Eastern Mediterranean. It was the great catalyst, the prime mover that withered the fields, emptied the granaries, and starved the empires from within. It turned the predictable rhythms of nature, upon which the entire palace economy was built, into a chaotic death march of famine and desperation.

This environmental shock exposed the second culprit: the inherent system fragility of the Glimmering World. The palace economies were marvels of centralized efficiency, but they were catastrophically brittle. They were optimized for stability and had no shock absorbers. The intricate, interdependent trade networks that brought tin from Afghanistan and amber from the Baltic were a source of immense wealth, but their very complexity made them vulnerable. A single broken link—a pirate raid, a city destroyed, a harbor silted up—could cascade through the entire system, causing a catastrophic failure. The world of the Great Kings was a beautiful and intricate machine, but it was a machine with no Plan B.

These two forces—climate change and system fragility—gave birth to the third: **mass migration**. The hungry and the desperate, uprooted from their withered lands in Greece, Anatolia, and the islands, took to the sea. They were not an army of conquest in the traditional sense; they were a wave of humanity, a confederation of the dispossessed, searching for a new home. Their oxcarts, filled with their families, are the most poignant evidence of their true nature. They were refugees armed with the fury of those who have nothing left to lose.

And finally, there was **technological disruption**. The old world was defined by bronze and the chariot. Both were expensive, elite technologies, requiring complex supply chains and state-level sponsorship. The chaos of the collapse broke those supply chains, making bronze a scarce luxury. In its place, a new, more democratic metal arose out of necessity: iron. Locally available and relatively cheap, iron would eventually arm new kinds of armies, citizen-soldiers who did not depend on the patronage of a palace. The collapse swept away the age of the Chariot Kings and ushered in the Iron Age, a new world with new rules of warfare and new social possibilities.

This, then, is the anatomy of the first great systems collapse. It was a convergence, a fatal synergy of environmental disaster, economic fragility, social upheaval, and technological change. No single factor can explain the totality of the destruction. It was the storm of all storms, and it left behind a world that was smaller, poorer, and darker.

And yet, our story did not end in the darkness. It ended with the glimmers of a new dawn. This is the final, and perhaps most important, lesson of the Bronze Age Collapse. It is a story of profound loss, but it is also a testament to the extraordinary resilience of the human spirit. Collapse is a filter, a brutal pruning of the old and inflexible, but it is also a catalyst for radical innovation.

From the ashes of the Mycenaean palaces, the memory of heroes survived in the songs of bards, planting the seeds for the future glories of classical Greece. From the ranks of the defeated Peleset invaders, a new nation of Philistines arose, building a powerful and sophisticated state on the coast of Canaan. From the highlands of the interior, a collection of tribes coalesced around the revolutionary idea of a single, universal God, an idea that would change the spiritual history of the world. And from the sheltered harbors of the surviving Canaanite cities, the Phoenician merchants emerged, not only reconnecting the shattered world with their trade, but giving it the transformative gift of the alphabet.

The end of one world was the beginning of many.

CONCLUSION

It is impossible to walk through these ancient ruins, to read these last, desperate letters, and not hear the echoes in our own time. We too live in a globalized, interconnected world of immense complexity. We too are dependent on intricate, fragile supply chains that bring us everything from the food we eat to the phones in our pockets. We too face the undeniable reality of a rapidly changing climate, with the prospect of droughts, famines, and extreme weather events that threaten our stability. And we too are witnessing mass migrations of desperate peoples, fleeing conflict, poverty, and environmental disaster.

The story of the Bronze Age Collapse is not a prophecy. History does not repeat itself, not exactly. But it does rhyme. It offers a powerful cautionary tale, a 3,000-year-old case study in what can happen when a complex society is pushed beyond its limits. It reminds us that our own glittering civilization, for all its technological prowess, is not immune to the same forces that brought down the Chariot Kings. Our world, too, has its own systemic fragilities, its own unseen rust in the gears.

But if the collapse is a warning, it is also a source of a strange and powerful hope. It shows us that humanity survives. It adapts. It innovates. It remembers. It proves that even in the darkest of ages, the human capacity to rebuild, to create new social forms, new technologies, and new ideas, is never extinguished.

The world of the Bronze Age is gone, but it is not silent. It speaks to us from the burned ruins of its cities, from the treasures in its sunken ships, and from the last words on its clay tablets. It tells us that we are not the first globalized civilization to face a systemic crisis. It warns us of the dangers of ignoring the fragility of our own interconnected world.

And it reminds us that the choices we make in the face of our own converging storms will echo for millennia to come. The long shadow of the past is upon us. It is up to us to decide whether we will be the ones to finally heed its lessons.

Dramatis Personae

The history of the Late Bronze Age is a sprawling drama played out across a vast stage by a cast of powerful and often larger-than-life characters. Here is a brief guide to the key players—the kings, queens, officials, and peoples who appear in this story.

The Egyptian Pharaohs

Ramesses III (reigned c. 1186–1155 B.C.)

The central figure of the collapse narrative and the self-proclaimed savior of Egypt. It is on the walls of his mortuary temple at Medinet Habu that we find the most detailed depiction of the Sea Peoples. His reign marks a great military victory but also the beginning of Egypt's long, slow decline and the end of its time as a world power.

Ramesses II, "The Great" (reigned c. 1279–1213 B.C.)

The most powerful and famous pharaoh of the New Kingdom, who reigned for an astonishing 67 years. He was a master builder and propagandist. He fought the Hittite

King Muwatalli II at the Battle of Kadesh and later signed the world's first-known peace treaty with Hattusili III. He represents the peak of Egyptian imperial power before the decline.

Merneptah (reigned c. 1213–1203 B.C.)

The son and successor of Ramesses II. He faced the *first* great wave of invaders from the sea—a coalition of Libyans and Sea Peoples (including the Ekwesh and Shekelesh). His victory stela provides crucial early evidence for the growing crisis and contains the first known historical mention of "Israel."

Akhenaten (reigned c. 1353–1336 B.C.)

The "Heretic Pharaoh." He abandoned Egypt's traditional pantheon to worship a single deity, the sun-disk Aten. He moved his capital to the new city of Akhetaten (modern Amarna), the site where the invaluable Amarna Letters were discovered. His inward-looking religious revolution created a power vacuum that the Hittites skillfully exploited.

Amenhotep III (reigned c. 1391–1353 B.C.)

Father of Akhenaten. His reign represents the absolute zenith of the Glimmering World's prosperity and diplomatic stability. The early Amarna Letters, sent to his court, depict a powerful and confident king at the center of the "Great Club."

The Hittite Great Kings

Šuppiluliuma II (reigned c. 1207–1178 B.C.)

The last known king of the Hittite Empire. He inherited a kingdom already crumbling from famine and rebellion. His desperate, unanswered pleas for grain shipments from Ugarit are a poignant testament to the empire's final, agonizing moments before it vanished from history.

Hattusili III (reigned c. 1267–1237 B.C.)

The Hittite king who, after years of conflict, negotiated and signed the landmark peace treaty with Ramesses II, formally ending the hostilities that had culminated at Kadesh. He represents the last great era of diplomatic stability between the two superpowers.

Muwatalli II (reigned c. 1295–1272 B.C.)

The shrewd and experienced opponent of Ramesses II at the Battle of Kadesh. He masterminded the brilliant military trap that nearly destroyed the Egyptian army, securing a strategic victory for the Hittites even if he lost the subsequent propaganda war.

Šuppiluliuma I (reigned c. 1344–1322 B.C.)

A cunning and ambitious Hittite king who took full advantage of Akhenaten's negligence. He shattered the rival kingdom of Mitanni and massively expanded Hittite power in Syria, transforming the political landscape and setting the stage for the great superpower rivalry with Egypt.

Other Kings and Rulers

Ammurapi (reigned c. 1215–1185 B.C.)

The last king of the wealthy port city of Ugarit. A loyal vassal of the Hittites, he sent his army and fleet away to aid his overlord, leaving his own kingdom defenseless. His final, frantic letters, preserved in a palace kiln, provide a harrowing, real-time account of his city's destruction by the Sea Peoples.

Tushratta (reigned c. 1382-1342 B.C.)

The king of Mitanni, a major power that was being squeezed between the Hittites and Assyrians. His letters in the Amarna archive are a desperate attempt to maintain his alliance with Egypt, offering his daughter as a bride while complaining bitterly about the quality of the gold he received in return.

Rib-Hadda (14th century B.C.)

The long-suffering ruler of the port city of Byblos. He was a loyal vassal of Egypt, but his sixty-plus pleading letters to the Pharaoh Akhenaten, begging for help against his rivals and the encroaching *Habiru*, went largely unanswered. His story is a perfect case study of the breakdown of imperial control.

The Peoples of the Sea and the Dispossessed

The Sea Peoples

The collective name given by the Egyptians to the confederation of seafaring raiders and migrants who attacked the Eastern Mediterranean at the end of the Bronze Age. They were not a single ethnic group, but a coalition of different peoples displaced by the widespread collapse.

The Peleset

The most prominent group within the Sea Peoples coalition, identifiable by their distinctive "feathered" headdresses. After their defeat by Ramesses III, they were settled on the coast of Canaan, where they became the Philistines of the Hebrew Bible.

The Sherden

Fierce warriors known for their horned helmets and long swords. They operated as both pirates and elite mercenaries, serving in the armies of Ramesses II and III even as their kinsmen fought against Egypt as part of the Sea Peoples coalition.

The *Habiru* (or *'Apiru*)

A term for the outcasts of Bronze Age society. Not an ethnic group, but a social class of landless refugees, runaway servants, and outlaws who lived on the fringes of the palace economies. Their numbers swelled during the collapse, and they became a major destabilizing force from within.

Timeline of Collapse

A Note on Ancient Chronology: All dates for this period are approximate and subject to scholarly debate. The dates provided here represent a general consensus and are intended to give a sequential framework for the events discussed in this book. The use of "c." (circa) indicates an approximate date.

Part I: The Glimmering World at its Zenith (c. 1400–1250 B.C.)

This period represents the height of the Late Bronze Age international system, characterized by a balance of power between great empires, unprecedented prosperity, and a complex network of global trade.

- c. 1391–1353 B.C. – Reign of **Amenhotep III** in Egypt. His reign marks a high point of wealth, artistic achievement, and international diplomacy. The early **Amarna Letters** show him at the center of the "Great Club" of kings.
- c. 1353–1336 B.C. – Reign of **Akhenaten**, the "Heretic Pharaoh," in Egypt. His inward-looking religious revolution disrupts Egyptian foreign policy, creating a power vacuum in the Levant that the Hittite king **Šuppiluliuma**

I skillfully exploits.
- **c. 1344–1322 B.C.** – Reign of **Šuppiluliuma I** of the Hittites. He conquers the rival Kingdom of Mitanni, massively expands Hittite influence in Syria, and elevates the Hittite Empire to true superpower status, setting the stage for the great rivalry with Egypt.
- **c. 1330 B.C.** – Approximate date of the **Uluburun Shipwreck** off the coast of Turkey. The ship's astonishingly diverse cargo provides a perfect snapshot of the interconnected Bronze Age trade network at its peak.
- **c. 1279–1213 B.C.** – The long and influential reign of **Ramesses II ("The Great")** in Egypt.
- **c. 1274 B.C.** – **The Battle of Kadesh**. Ramesses II and the Hittite king Muwatalli II fight the largest known chariot battle in history to a bloody stalemate over the strategic city of Kadesh in Syria.
- **c. 1259 B.C.** – The **"Eternal Treaty"** is signed between Ramesses II and the new Hittite king, Hattusili III. The world's first-known comprehensive peace treaty, it establishes a formal defensive alliance between the two superpowers and ushers in a period of relative stability.
- **c. 1250 B.C.** – Major Mycenaean palaces in Greece (Mycenae, Tiryns, Pylos) begin a massive expansion of their fortifications, including the construction of Cyclopean walls and secret underground cisterns, suggesting a growing sense of widespread insecurity.

Part II: The Gathering Storm (c. 1250–1200 B.C.)

A period of growing instability, where the interlocking systems of the Bronze Age begin to fray under the pressure of environmental, social, and military crises.

- **c. 1250 B.C. onwards** – Paleoclimatological data (pollen, lakebed, and ice-core analysis) indicates the beginning of a severe, multi-decade **megadrought** across the Eastern Mediterranean and Near East, leading to widespread crop failures and famine, particularly in rain-fed agricultural regions like Greece and Anatolia.
- **c. 1225–1175 B.C.** – A proposed **"earthquake storm"** rocks the region. Archaeological evidence shows a sequence of major seismic events that destroy or severely damage key cities, including Troy (Troy VIh), Mycenae, Tiryns, Kition, and Ugarit.
- **c. 1213–1203 B.C.** – Reign of Pharaoh **Merneptah** in Egypt.
- **c. 1208 B.C.** – Merneptah defeats a major invasion of the western Delta by a coalition of Libyan tribes and the first-named confederation of Sea Peoples, including the **Ekwesh**, **Teresh**, **Lukka**, and **Shekelesh**. His victory stela provides the first clear evidence of large-scale, migrating groups from "the countries of the sea" and also contains the first known historical reference to "Israel" in Canaan.
- **c. 1207 B.C.** – Accession of **Šuppiluliuma II**, the last known king of the Hittite Empire. He inherits an empire already facing catastrophic famine and rebellion.
- **Late 13th Century B.C.** – Hittite kings make desperate pleas for grain shipments from their vassals. A letter from the Hittite court found at Ugarit declares a famine situation to be a **"matter of life and death."**

Part III: The Great Unraveling (c. 1200–1175 B.C.)

The catastrophic climax of the collapse, a period of just one or two generations in which the great palace centers are violently destroyed and entire civilizations vanish.

- **c. 1200 B.C.** – A major horizon of destruction across the Mycenaean world. The **Palace of Nestor at Pylos** is violently destroyed by fire. Its final Linear B tablets, baked in the conflagration, detail a kingdom frantically preparing for a coastal invasion that it could not repel.
- **c. 1190 B.C.** – The great citadels of **Mycenae** and **Tiryns** suffer their final, fiery destruction, marking the definitive end of the Mycenaean palace civilization. The knowledge of Linear B writing is lost, and Greece enters a "Dark Age."
- **c. 1185 B.C.** – The wealthy port city of **Ugarit** on the Syrian coast is violently destroyed. Its final, desperate letters—preserved in a kiln—document the city being stripped of its troops and fleet by its Hittite overlord just as an unnamed enemy fleet appears offshore.
- **c. 1180 B.C.** – The Hittite capital of **Hattusa** is destroyed by fire and permanently abandoned. The Hittite Empire, a superpower for over 400 years, effectively ceases to exist.
- **c. 1178 B.C.** – The great land and sea battles between Pharaoh **Ramesses III** and a second, larger Sea Peoples confederation, including the **Peleset, Tjekker, Shekelesh, Denyen,** and **Weshesh**. Ramesses wins a decisive victory, halting their advance into Egypt.
- **c. 1175 B.C.** – Ramesses III settles defeated Peleset and other Sea Peoples as garrison troops in fortified cities on the southern coast of Canaan. This act leads to the birth

of **Philistia** and the Philistine Pentapolis (Gaza, Ashkelon, Ashdod, Ekron, Gath).

Part IV: Out of the Ashes (c. 1175 B.C. and beyond)

The long aftermath, characterized by a smaller, poorer, and more fragmented world, but also by resilience, adaptation, and the innovations that would define the subsequent Iron Age.

- **c. 1159 B.C.** – The **first recorded labor strike in history** occurs at Deir el-Medina in Egypt, as the craftsmen of the royal tombs protest against the state's failure to deliver their grain rations, signaling deep economic trouble even within victorious Egypt.
- **c. 1155 B.C.** – Pharaoh **Ramesses III** is assassinated in a palace conspiracy known as the "Harem Conspiracy."
- **c. 1150–750 B.C.** – The **Greek Dark Age**. A period of profound population decline, poverty, isolation, and illiteracy following the collapse of the Mycenaean civilization. Oral tradition, particularly the stories that would form the basis of the Homeric epics, keeps the memory of the Bronze Age alive.
- **c. 1100 B.C.** – The Egyptian text, the **"Story of Wenamun,"** is written. It vividly illustrates the new political reality of Egyptian weakness and the rise of independent city-states like Phoenician Byblos.
- **c. 1050 B.C.** – The fully developed 22-letter **Phoenician alphabet** emerges, a simple and efficient script that would revolutionize communication.
- **c. 1000 B.C.** – The rise of the **Israelite Monarchy** under

Kings Saul and David, largely as a centralized response to the military and political pressure from the powerful Philistine city-states on the coast.
- **c. 9th–8th Centuries B.C.** – Phoenician mariners establish a vast network of trading colonies across the Mediterranean, from Cyprus to Spain.
- **c. 814 B.C.** – Traditional date for the founding of **Carthage** by Phoenician colonists from Tyre.
- **c. 750 B.C.** – The end of the Greek Dark Age. The **Homeric epics**, the *Iliad* and the *Odyssey*, are composed and written down for the first time as the Greeks adopt and adapt the Phoenician alphabet, adding vowels and creating a true phonetic script.

A Curated Visual Archive for the Late Bronze Age Collapse

Part I: The Apogee of a Globalized World

The Late Bronze Age (c. 1550-1200 BCE) was characterized by a sophisticated and deeply interconnected international system. The great powers of the day—the Egyptian New Kingdom, the Hittite Empire, the Mycenaean palace-states, and the Kingdom of Mitanni—formed an exclusive "Great Club" of rulers who communicated as peers, traded vast quantities of goods, and engaged in both high-stakes diplomacy and monumental warfare. The following images showcase the wealth, power, and complexity of this first great globalized era.

Section 1.1: The Great Club: Diplomacy and Dynasties

The engine of the LBA international system was diplomacy, conducted through a shared language and a set of common protocols. This was not a system of abstract treaties but one built on the tangible and often personal exchange of luxury goods, precious metals, and people—specifically, the royal women who served as the human currency of political alliances.

An Amarna Letter (EA 23)

A letter from the Amarna archive (EA 23), sent by King Tushratta of Mitanni to Pharaoh Amenhotep III, discussing the sending of a statue of the goddess Šauška to Egypt for the pharaoh's health and referencing Tushratta's daughter, Tadu-Hepa, who was a wife in the Egyptian court. Licensed under the Creative Commons Attribution-Share Alike 4.0 International License.

Bust of Nefertiti

The famous bust of Nefertiti, chief wife of Akhenaten, c. 1345 BCE. Some scholars have theorized that the Mitannian princess Tadu-Hepa, sent to Egypt as a diplomatic bride, may have been this very same, powerful woman. Photo by Philip Pikart courtesy of Wikimedia Commons.

Section 1.2: The Citadel Kings: Power and Administration in Mycenaean Greece

In the Aegean, the dominant powers were the Mycenaean palace-states of mainland Greece. Centered in massive, heavily fortified citadels, these kingdoms were ruled by a king, or *wanax*, who presided over a highly centralized and bureaucratic administration. Their power was projected through monumental architecture and maintained by an obsessive system of economic control.

The Lion Gate at Mycenae

The Lion Gate, the main entrance to the citadel of Mycenae, c. 1250 BCE. The massive stones, or "Cyclopean masonry," were believed by later Greeks to have been built by giants. Licensed under the Creative Commons Attribution-Share Alike 4.0 International License.

A Linear B Tablet

A Linear B tablet from the Palace of Nestor at Pylos, c. 1180 BCE. This tablet, preserved when the palace burned, meticulously inventories vessels, including several bronze tripods, demonstrating the obsessive accounting of the palace economy. Licensed under the Creative Commons Attribution-Share Alike 4.0 International License.

Section 1.3: Masters of the Wine-Dark Sea

The LBA was an age of maritime trade on an unprecedented scale. Raw materials and finished goods moved across the Mediterranean in ships laden with cargoes sourced from a dozen or more distinct cultures. The single greatest piece of evidence for this interconnected maritime world is the Uluburun shipwreck.

The Uluburun Shipwreck Artifacts

A portion of the recovered cargo from the Uluburun shipwreck, displayed at the Bodrum Museum of Underwater Archaeology. The find included over ten tons of copper, a ton of tin, glass ingots, pottery, and luxury goods from across the ancient world. Licensed under the Creative Commons Attribution-Share Alike 4.0 International License.

Section 1.4: The Chariot Kings

The defining military technology of the Late Bronze Age was the light, two-wheeled war chariot. It was a revolutionary weapon system that dominated the battlefields of the Near East for centuries. The ability to field and maintain large chariot corps was the measure of a Great King's power, and the image of the pharaoh as an invincible charioteer became the ultimate expression of royal propaganda.

Relief of the Battle of Kadesh

The Battle of Kadesh as propaganda: Ramesses II, depicted as a superhuman figure, charges into the chaotic Hittite chariot corps. This relief, carved at Abu Simbel, cemented the pharaoh's preferred narrative of a heroic personal victory. Licensed under the Creative Commons Attribution-Share Alike 4.0 International License.

Egyptian Chariot Model

A lightweight war chariot from the tomb of Tutankhamun, c. 1325 BCE. A masterpiece of composite construction, it was designed for speed and stability as a mobile archery platform. Licensed under the Creative Commons Attribution-Share Alike 4.0 International License.

Part II: The Storm: A World Unravels

Around 1200 BCE, the sophisticated, globalized world of the Late Bronze Age came to a sudden and violent end. In the space of a few decades, great empires fell, major cities were burned, trade routes were severed, and literacy was lost across vast regions. This "Great Unraveling" was not the result of a single cause but a "perfect storm" of cascading and interconnected crises, including climate change, earthquakes, internal rebellions, and the mass migrations of displaced peoples.

Section 2.1: The Collapse Cascade: Destruction, Depopulation, and Disruption

The archaeological record of the 12th century BCE is written in fire and rubble. Across the Eastern Mediterranean, from Greece to Anatolia and the Levant, destruction layers mark the end of the palatial civilizations. The evidence points to a complex web of causes, where natural disasters may have weakened states, leaving them vulnerable to internal strife and external attack.

The "Earthquake Storm" (Collapsed Walls at Tiryns)

The collapsed walls of Tiryns. Evidence of widespread destruction at sites across the Aegean and Anatolia has led some scholars to propose an "earthquake storm"—a series of major seismic events that may have destabilized the region and triggered the collapse. Licensed under the Creative Commons Attribution-Share Alike 4.0 International License.

The "Warrior Vase"

A CURATED VISUAL ARCHIVE FOR THE LATE BRONZE AGE COLLAPSE

The "Warrior Vase," a krater from Mycenae dating to the 12th century BCE. The depiction of uniform, anonymous soldiers, a stark contrast to earlier heroic art, suggests a society on a permanent war footing right before its final collapse. Licensed under the Creative Commons Attribution-Share Alike 4.0 International License.

Section 2.2: The Northern Fury: The Sea Peoples Invasion

The most famous agents of the Late Bronze Age Collapse are the enigmatic "Sea Peoples." This term, coined by 19th-century scholars, is based on Egyptian inscriptions that describe a coalition of foreign peoples who attacked Egypt and the Levant by land and sea. The Egyptian records, particularly the reliefs at Medinet Habu, are our primary source for their appearance, tactics, and nature.

The Naval Battle Relief at Medinet Habu

The great naval battle against the Sea Peoples, as depicted by Ramesses III at Medinet Habu, c. 1175 BCE. Note the orderly Egyptian ships on the left trapping the chaotic, sail-driven ships of the invaders. Licensed under the Creative Commons Attribution-Share Alike 4.0 International License.

Relief of the Sherden Mercenaries (Horned Helmets)

A captive Sherden warrior, identifiable by his horned helmet, from the reliefs at Medinet Habu. The Sherden's shifting role—first as enemies of Egypt, then as elite mercenaries for the pharaoh, then as enemies once more—highlights the fluid allegiances of the collapsing Bronze Age world. Licensed under the Creative Commons Attribution-Share Alike 4.0 International License.

List: The Sea Peoples as Documented in Egyptian Records

The identities of the groups collectively known as the "Sea Peoples" are known almost exclusively from Egyptian records. This list serves as a concise guide to these enigmatic tribes.

Guide:
- Name (Egyptian Transliteration)
- Key Egyptian Source(s)
- Common Scholarly Identification / Notes

Peleset (prst)
Medinet Habu (Ramesses III)
Universally identified with the **Philistines**, who settled the southern coast of Canaan. Their feathered headdress is their key identifier.

Tjekker (tkr)
Medinet Habu, Story of Wenamun
A close ally of the Peleset, also wearing a feathered headdress. They settled at Dor on the Canaanite coast.

Sherden (s'rdn)
Amarna Letters, Kadesh, Medinet Habu
Identified by their horned helmets. Served as both enemies and elite mercenaries for Egypt. Possible connection to **Sardinia**.

Shekelesh (sˇkrsˇ)
Merneptah Stele, Medinet Habu
Origins are highly debated. Some scholars suggest a connection to **Sicily** based on the similar-sounding name.

Lukka (rkw)
Amarna Letters, Kadesh Inscriptions
Almost certainly from the **Lukka Lands** in southwestern Anatolia, the region known in the Classical era as **Lycia**.

Denyen (dny(n))
Medinet Habu
Often identified with the *Danuna* from the Amarna letters. Some scholars connect them to the Greek **Danaans** (a Homeric name for Greeks) or the Israelite Tribe of **Dan**.

Weshesh (wsˇsˇ)
Medinet Habu
Identity completely unknown. Name is a hapax legomenon (appears only once).

Ekwesh (jḳwsˇ)
Merneptah Stele
Described as being circumcised, which is unusual. Often identified with the **Achaeans** (Hittite: *Ahhiyawa*), a major group of Mycenaean Greeks.

Teresh (trsˇ)
Merneptah Stele
Sometimes connected to the *Tyrsenoi*, a name later used by Greeks for the **Etruscans** of Italy, though this is highly

speculative.

Conclusion

The visual archive presented in this report tells a dramatic story of a world built and a world lost. From this collapse, a new world was born. The destruction of the centralized, top-heavy palace systems created a power vacuum in which new peoples, like the Philistines, could forge new identities, and new, more adaptable technologies, like the alphabet, could flourish. The images from the aftermath tell a story not just of destruction, but of resilience and transformation. The legacy of the Bronze Age Collapse is therefore twofold: it is a cautionary tale about the fragility of even the most complex civilizations, and it is a testament to the human capacity for innovation and renewal in the face of catastrophe.

A Note On Sources

The story told in this book is a work of synthesis, an attempt to weave together decades of scholarship from multiple fields—archaeology, climatology, philology, and history—into a single, coherent narrative. While I have taken liberties in imagining the thoughts of a scribe or the terror of a citizen in a burning city, the historical scaffolding is built upon a foundation of hard evidence and the brilliant, painstaking work of countless scholars. For those who wish to dig deeper into this fascinating and mysterious period, what follows is a guide to the key primary sources and the modern works that have most profoundly shaped our understanding of the Late Bronze Age Collapse.

Primary Sources: The Voices of the Lost World

The bedrock of any history is the testimony of the past itself. For the Late Bronze Age, we are blessed with a handful of remarkable textual and archaeological discoveries that provide a direct window into their world.

- **The Amarna Letters:** The 382 clay tablets discovered at Tell el-Amarna in Egypt are our single most important source for understanding the international system at its peak. They are the diplomatic correspondence of the

great kings, raw, personal, and endlessly fascinating. The definitive English translation is William L. Moran's *The Amarna Letters* (1992).
- **The Medinet Habu Inscriptions:** The monumental reliefs and inscriptions of Ramesses III are the primary, if heavily biased, account of the Sea Peoples' invasions. The full texts can be found in the multi-volume *Epigraphic Survey, Medinet Habu* (1930–1970) by the Oriental Institute of the University of Chicago. For an accessible summary and analysis, many of the books listed below are invaluable.
- **The Linear B Tablets:** The administrative records from the Mycenaean palaces of Pylos, Mycenae, and Knossos provide a stunningly detailed, if dry, snapshot of the palace economy. The story of their decipherment by Michael Ventris is a tale in itself, brilliantly told in Andrew Robinson's *The Man Who Deciphered Linear B: The Story of Michael Ventris* (2002). John Chadwick's *The Mycenaean World* (1976) remains a classic and accessible introduction to the world revealed by the tablets.
- **The Ugaritic Texts:** The archives from the port city of Ugarit are a treasure trove, containing not only the last, frantic letters detailing the city's destruction, but also magnificent literary works like the *Baal Cycle* and the *Epic of Kirta*, which are our primary sources for understanding Canaanite religion. A good, accessible translation is Mark S. Smith's *The Ugaritic Baal Cycle: Volume I & II* (1994, 2009).
- **The Uluburun Shipwreck:** While not a text, the shipwreck itself is a primary source of unparalleled importance. The official publications are dense and academic, but the work of the Institute of Nautical Archaeology

(INA) is accessible through their website and various articles. The final report, edited by Cemal Pulak, provides exhaustive detail on the cargo and its implications for Bronze Age trade.

The Modern Investigation: Essential Reading

The following books represent some of the most important modern scholarship on the Late Bronze Age Collapse. They range from popular narratives to more academic studies, but all have been crucial in shaping the story you have just read.

The Foundational Narratives & Overviews:

- **Cline, Eric H. *1177 B.C.: The Year Civilization Collapsed* (2014, revised 2021).** This is, without question, the single most important and accessible book on the topic for a general audience. Cline masterfully synthesizes the complex evidence for a "perfect storm" of failures. My own book owes an immense intellectual debt to his work and its brilliant framing of the collapse as a systems failure. It is the perfect next step for any reader.
- **Drews, Robert. *The End of the Bronze Age: Changes in Warfare and the Catastrophe ca. 1200 B.C.* (1993).** A classic and highly influential, if now somewhat debated, work. Drews was one of the first to propose a single, overarching cause for the collapse, arguing that a revolutionary change in warfare—the advent of massed infantry with new types of weaponry—rendered the chariot-based armies of the great kings obsolete. While the "perfect storm" model is now more widely accepted, Drews's focus on military

technology remains essential.
- **Sandars, N.K. *The Sea Peoples: Warriors of the Ancient Mediterranean, 1250-1150 BC* (1978).** The original popular synthesis on the topic. Though some of its specific theories have been superseded by new discoveries, Sandars's work remains a beautifully written and evocative introduction to the mystery, and she was one of the first to treat the Sea Peoples as a complex phenomenon rather than a simple barbarian horde.

On Specific Cultures and Regions:

- **Bryce, Trevor. *The Kingdom of the Hittites* (New Edition, 2005).** The definitive and most readable history of the Hittite Empire. His chapters on the final decades and the "phantom empire's" collapse are particularly masterful and informed my own reconstruction of those events.
- **Dickinson, Oliver. *The Aegean Bronze Age* (1994).** A comprehensive and authoritative survey of the Mycenaean and Minoan worlds. It is an indispensable guide to the archaeology, art, and social structure of the civilization that would later be immortalized by Homer.
- **Aubet, Maria Eugenia. *The Phoenicians and the West: Politics, Colonies and Trade* (Second Edition, 2001).** The best single-volume work on the rise of the Phoenicians. Aubet brilliantly details their trade networks, their colonial expansion, and their cultural innovations in the wake of the Bronze Age collapse.
- **Dothan, Trude, and Moshe Dothan. *People of the Sea: The Search for the Philistines* (1992).** A fascinating

account of the archaeology of the Philistines, written by two of the pioneering excavators of their sites. It clearly lays out the evidence for their Aegean origins and their cultural development in their new Canaanite home.
- **Finkelstein, Israel, and Neil Asher Silberman.** *The Bible Unearthed: Archaeology's New Vision of Ancient Israel and the Origin of Its Sacred Texts* **(2001).** A groundbreaking and controversial work that uses archaeology to reconstruct the history of ancient Israel. Their chapters on the emergence of Israel in the central hill country during the Iron Age, and its relationship with the Philistines, provide a crucial historical context for the biblical narratives.

On Climate, Systems Collapse, and the Bigger Picture:

- **Broodbank, Cyprian.** *The Making of the Middle Sea: A History of the Mediterranean from the Beginning to the Emergence of the Classical World* **(2013).** A magisterial and sweeping history of the entire Mediterranean. His chapters on the "First International Age" and its subsequent collapse are brilliant in their scope, placing the events we have discussed into a much larger geographical and chronological context.
- **Drake, Brandon L. "The influence of climatic change on the Late Bronze Age Collapse and the Greek Dark Ages." (*Journal of Archaeological Science*, 2012).** For those interested in the hard science, this academic paper provides an excellent overview of the paleoclimatological evidence for the megadrought and its direct impact on the civilizations of the Eastern Mediterranean.

- **Tainter, Joseph A. *The Collapse of Complex Societies* (1988).** A seminal theoretical work in the field of "collapsology." Tainter argues that societies collapse when their investment in complexity reaches a point of diminishing returns. While not focused specifically on the Bronze Age, his analytical framework for understanding *why* complex systems fail is an essential intellectual tool for making sense of the events in this book.

This list is by no means exhaustive, but it represents the broad shoulders of the giants—historians, archaeologists, and scientists—upon which this narrative stands. Their work has rescued this pivotal moment in human history from the realm of myth and transformed it into a powerful, and deeply relevant, story for our own time.

Printed in Dunstable, United Kingdom